Praise for

RAISING TEENS WHO TALK TO YOU

Raising Teens Who Talk to You is a wise and deeply compassionate guide that recognizes how we relate to ourselves influences how we relate to our children. Blending science, real-life experience, and practical guidance from dozens of experts, it helps parents navigate conflict, big emotions, and today's complex challenges with greater presence and care. This is not just a book about raising teenagers; it's an invitation to practice self-compassion as the foundation for connection, trust, and a relationship with your teens that can grow and endure over time.

—**Dr. Kristin Neff**, researcher, author of *Self-Compassion* and *Fierce Self-Compassion*

Cecilia and Jason have brought together a thoughtful group of voices to explore what it really looks like to stay connected through the complexity of adolescence and beyond. This book offers perspective, reassurance, and practical insight, making it a meaningful resource for parents who want to stay focused on connection and build a relationship that lasts a lifetime.

—**Cathy Cassani Adams**, LCSW, social worker, author of *Restoring Our Girls: How Real Conversations Shape Our Daughters' Lives, Help Them with Teen Challenges,* and *Remind Them That They Matter*

Exactly the book that the parents I work with are asking for, and the teens I work with wish their parents had. So many unique perspectives and voices make this book accessible to many parents with different kinds of concerns. Highly recommend this one for your bedside table!
—**Dr. Chris Willard**, Harvard Medical School, clinical psychologist, author of *Growing Up Mindful*

It's absolutely possible to enjoy your teen and stay deeply connected, even through tough times. Whether you're working to rebuild that closeness or hold onto it, *Raising Teens Who Talk to You* has your back.
—**Tosha Schore**, author of *Listen: Five Simple Tools to Meet Your Everyday Parenting Challenges*, founder of Parenting Boys Peacefully

I love that this book doesn't just tell parents what to do; it invites them to look inward first. That's where lasting change actually begins.
—**Jennifer Smith Miller**, author of *Confident Parents, Confident Kids*, parent coach, expert to NBC Education Nation's Parent Toolkit

The teen years ask something of parents that nobody really warns you about. They ask you to grow. This book meets that ask beautifully—centering the relationship, inviting real self-awareness, and not shying away from the hard parts. Cecilia and Jason have built something truly valuable and generous here. I'm glad it exists.
—**Dr. Carrie Contey**, psychologist, parenting coach, author

Raising Teens Who Talk to You is a reflective and empowering journey through the lived experiences of fellow parents turned experts. Sharing valuable lessons through their relatable stories, our own parenting challenges are reframed with compassion and understanding. This collection of authors creates the community in which you want to raise your teen; each chapter is the open arms you can return to when you need support.

—**Arleen Tyndall**, BScPhm, ACPR, Dr. Shefali-trained conscious parenting and life coach, author of "A Mirror of Inherited Pain," *The Perfectly Imperfect Family*

The landscape our teens navigate today is completely different from the one we grew up in. This is a timely compendium of wisdom to give parents of teens the skills and the information they need to help their kids stay safe, stay happy, and become real-world ready. I have supported generations of children and families from a safeguarding standpoint in schools, and I can say hands down that the section on Dealing with Sex, Drugs, and Runaway Digital is unmissable for parents. We all typically worry that we will say the wrong thing at the wrong time regarding these weapons-grade issues. Here, experts give us the whys and hows with clarity and compassion. It's a go-to resource that meets parents at urgent points of need when childhood and teen-dom are fast-tracked via the digital world.

—**Emma Gleadhil**, education consultant, parenting coach, author

If you are parenting a tween or teenager, this book is a must-read. It beautifully articulates what I believe is one of the most important parenting tools we have: connection. With a thoughtful balance of lived experience and professional insight, it offers practical guidance to help parents stay steady, connected, and present through the complexity of the teen years.

—**Dr. Natasha Ching**, FRACP, MBBS, pediatrician, author and co-host of *Mum to Mum with Doctor Tash*

This is the kind of parenting support so many of us are craving right now—real, grounded, and rooted in connection, not control. *Raising Teens Who Talk to You* gently reminds us that when we regulate ourselves and create safety at home, our teens are far more likely to stay open and connected. It's honest, practical, and feels like being guided by people who truly get it.

—**Dana Denning**, author, founder of Nourished Nest, holistic interior designer

RAISING TEENS WHO TALK TO YOU

A Connected Parenting Approach to Adolescence

CECILIA & JASON HILKEY
and other leading voices

Disclaimer:

The information in this book is provided for educational and informational purposes only. The parenting tips and conflict resolution strategies reflect the authors' personal experiences and opinions. What has worked for the authors may not be suitable for every family or situation.

Names, identifying details, and certain scenarios have been changed to protect the privacy of individuals involved in the stories shared throughout the book.

For serious family conflicts or behavioral issues, readers are encouraged to seek guidance from qualified professionals. The authors and publisher do not provide psychological or legal services and assume no responsibility for how this information is applied.

Summit Press Publishers
PO Box 1356
Intervale, New Hampshire 03845

First edition: May 2026
ISBN: 979-8-9939104-2-0

For information about special discounts available for bulk purchase, workshops, retreats, and webinars associated with this book, please contact us at support@HappilyFamily.com

TABLE OF CONTENTS

Section Two

The Inner Work of Parenting

Section Three

Hard Moments, Real Growth

Section Four

Dealing with Sex, Drugs & Runaway Digital

Section Five

Letting Go While Staying Close

BEFORE WE BEGIN

You want more for your teen.

You want to raise a teen who talks to you, but you want even more than that. You want a connection with your teen. You want to understand them and be understood.

You want them to share who they are—not just the safe, polished parts they show "when mom is around," but the tender spots too. You want to hear their hopes, struggles, doubts, and worries. Most of all, you want your teen to feel safe enough not to hide the parts that might disappoint you.

You want a teen who is thinking deeply about their life and the impact of their choices—not so they beat themselves up with regret or shame, but so they can learn and grow into an adult they are proud of.

You want your teen to strive, work hard, and persist in the face of setbacks, but also to recognize when a situation—be it a relationship, job, or commitment—is too painful or demanding and requires reconsideration.

You want your teen to have compassion for others, to be moved by people who have less, and to be responsive to the pain in the world. You also want your teen to include themselves in the compassion they extend to others.

You want a teen who listens not just to friends or loud voices on social media, but also to their own inner voice—not the loud, reactive one heard first, but the quieter wisdom that speaks second.

You want a teen who makes and keeps friends, responds to healthy feedback, but doesn't try to please everyone.

You want a resilient teen who can bounce back, recover, and adapt to an ever-changing world, while making decisions aligned with their (and your) values and being true to themselves.

You're in the right place.

If these things are true for you and what you want for your teen, then the book you are holding in your hands is a great place to start. Your child might already be a teen, or you might be preparing for the teen years. Either way, you're in the right place.

Welcome to the "New Adolescence"

If you're parenting a teen, chances are that you've noticed something: the teen years look different than they used to. We call this the "New Adolescence." We are referring to the phenomenon of the world changing so quickly that we have to parent our kids through experiences we didn't have when we were their age. Here are some aspects of the New Adolescence covered in future chapters.

Life Milestones Happen Later

In the United States—and likely other countries too—young adults are reaching life milestones later than previous generations did (such as finishing their education, becoming financially independent, getting

married, and having kids). There are certainly many factors that contribute to young people accomplishing things later than our generation did. So if you find yourself thinking, "When I was my child's age,
I'd done so much more by then," you're not wrong. Because of this
shift, parents are also parenting for more years, staying more involved
emotionally, and often financially, with their children.

Technology

Teens now grow up in a digital world unlike ours. From a young age,
they see people glued to devices in an always-on culture, with technology promising help and bringing disruption. Their world is more
polarized, unstable, and environmentally tenuous.

Adolescents today tend to be overprotected in the physical world,
but underprotected in the digital one. Kids are exposed to pornography at younger ages. Social media and tech companies have yet to put
meaningful safeguards in place for protecting the mental health of
adolescents, especially young girls, as well as safeguards for privacy
and data collection.

Mental Health and Neurodiversity

Due to the adolescent mental health crisis, more of our teens have
mental illnesses like anxiety or depression. Thankfully, the world our
children inhabit doesn't stigmatize neurodiversity, physical disability,
or mental illness like previous generations did, but these conditions
make growing up more complicated. In addition, more young people
have ADHD, autism, or neurodiversity than ever before. Sometimes

teens receive a formal diagnosis from a health professional, and some-times teens self-diagnose from social media. Regardless of where the diagnosis is coming from, the prevalence and acceptance of different conditions have increased, while the stigma has decreased for seeking out support, using medication, and going to therapy.

Cannabis

In the U.S., several states have legalized recreational cannabis for people 21 and up. This led to the development of cannabis with much higher levels of THC than ever before. While alcohol use is decreasing among teens, research shows that this high-potency cannabis is being used more frequently. Parents may think that cannabis is safer to use (and misuse) in comparison to alcohol, but it still carries significant risk. Early research warns that cannabis impacts a teen's developing brain during an especially critical period. Only time—and more research—will tell exactly how much this generation of teens was affected.

LGBTQ and Gender Identity

Our kids are growing up around more people who are LGBTQ. The world our kids inhabit is more gender diverse and accepting than previous generations. This could bring up all sorts of feelings for us parents. Depending on your situation and perspective, if your teen is exploring, questioning, or expressing their gender identity or sexual orientation, it could feel wonderful or worrisome.

It's Not Your Fault, But It Is Your Responsibility

Whatever is happening with your teen right now, parenting teens is arguably more complicated for us than for previous generations. You aren't responsible for the current state of the world; you didn't create the current conditions. The only choice any of us has is how we respond to these times, the relationship we build with our teen, and the kind of parent we become. Therein lies your power. And this is where things actually get exciting.

Raising Teens Who Talk to You is a parenting anthology built around one research-backed idea: the relationship between you and your teen is the most important factor in how adolescence unfolds. In the following pages, the authors will show you that your influence as a parent depends far more on your connection with your teen than on any rules or adult-imposed consequences.

This book is written by a diverse community of therapists, psychologists, coaches, educators, and parents. Inside 36 short chapters, you'll discover the full landscape of raising teenagers in the "New Adolescence," including what you need to know about the adolescent brain, doing your own inner work, how to survive and thrive during hard moments, how to handle "hot topics" like sex, drugs, and digital life, and the bittersweet task of letting go.

Each author brings their own voice, story, and specialty—so that, together, we can create something rare: a parenting book that feels less like a manual and more like sitting down with a wise, honest, deeply caring community of people who have been there.

Organized with You in Mind

You'll notice that the chapters are organized to take you on a journey, to get you from point A to Z, but that doesn't mean you have to start at the beginning. If you wake up at 3 a.m. and you're worried about something, feel free to jump to the chapter that addresses your concern. If you want to delve even deeper into that topic, feel free to scan the QR code at the end of the chapter, as many of the authors have additional free resources for parents looking for more support.

Section One: The Relationship as the Foundation. These chapters explain why the tools that worked when your kids were young suddenly stop working, what the developing adolescent brain actually needs, and how you can shift from managing behavior to building genuine connection. You'll get practical insight into listening without giving unsolicited advice, being curious (and why that's important), and repairing the relationship with your teen after a disconnection.

Section Two: The Inner Work of Parenting. One of the principles we've taught for a long time is that, before we parents can show up for our kids, we often need to do some self-reflection and healing. This section turns the lens inward. You'll see how to regulate your own nervous systems, process the emotions from your own adolescence, and create a home that feels like a sanctuary rather than a second job. The core message is that your most powerful parenting tools are self-regulation and self-awareness.

Section Three: Hard Moments, Real Growth. Here we talk about the tough moments of teen parenting—when emotions escalate, when a neurodivergent teen seems unreachable, when the weight of worry becomes too heavy to carry alone. You will see how to move from reacting to responding, how to sit with your teen's discomfort instead of rushing to fix it, and how to become the safe place your teen needs—especially in the moments when your teen is acting like they don't want you around.

Section Four: Dealing with Sex, Drugs, & Runaway Digital. You will discover how to have ongoing, shame-free conversations about sex, teen marijuana dependency, and smartphones. Each chapter pairs honest information with a connected, non-panicked approach to calm your anxiety, normalize the struggles many families are facing right now, and offer helpful advice for addressing these issues.

Section Five: Letting Go While Staying Close. The final section addresses the hardest truth of parenting teenagers: your job is to work yourself out of a job. Chapters will guide you through the shift from controlling behavior to becoming a partner with your teen, how to rebuild trust after it has been broken, supporting your neurodivergent teen's growing autonomy, and how to stay close through evolving identities—including LGBTQ teens navigating their sense of self.

We'll Meet You Where You Are

Jason and I created this book and brought together a community of authors because we had our own struggles as parents, especially when our kids became teens. Even though we've created Happily Family to support parents worldwide, even though we've conducted over 275 interviews with parenting authors, speakers, therapists, and researchers, and even though we've supported thousands of families, it doesn't mean our own teens were immune to the challenges of growing up. For us, those years were messy; we didn't have as much support as we wanted, and we couldn't find many current books or resources about raising teens. We attempted to be self-compassionate, but we also blamed ourselves for our children's struggles. We felt alone and ashamed. In our eyes, because our kids struggled, we had failed. Our wish for you is that your journey is a little smoother than ours was.

Wherever you are now, we'll meet you there. Speaking for all the authors, we want you to feel like we're all sitting together with you in your living room. We want you to feel supported and less alone. We're on your side—and your teen's side—we're cheering for you.

You don't need to show up perfectly. (You'll read a bunch of stories in here about the mistakes we've all made along the way.) If you mess up, you can repair and reconnect with your teen. It's never too late.

And if you find yourself off course, trust your own inner wisdom, listen to your own inner voice—not the loud, reactive internal voice that you may hear first—but the quieter wisdom that often speaks second.

All Our Love,
Cecilia and Jason Hilkey

SECTION ONE

THE RELATIONSHIP AS THE FOUNDATION

———

STILL GROUNDED

Melanie Zwyghuizen

I'm fifty-six years old, and I'm still grounded.

At sixteen, my dad announced my sentence: "You're grounded until you're sixty."

Four more years to go.

He thought he'd won. He thought he had control.

What he actually had was a daughter who became an expert liar and rarely got caught.

I didn't sneak in late because I was a bad kid. I did it because I'd learned through the years that honesty was costly. That sharing my real life meant lectures, punishment, and disappointed looks that made me feel fundamentally broken. So I split myself in two: the compliant daughter my parents saw at dinner, and the actual teenager I was the moment their backs were turned.

My dad could control my curfew. He could control whether I left the house. He could take my car keys, ground me until retirement age, pile on consequences until I graduated high school and beyond. And he did.

Here's what I learned that my dad never did: Control gets you compliance in the moment. Influence gets you connection that lasts a lifetime.

My dad had all the control he thought he needed, but he didn't have influence.

He might have had wisdom to offer me. He might have helped me navigate those identity questions, those moments of doubt, that search for belonging. But I'll never know. Because I didn't want to hear a single word he had to say.

No one wants to accept guidance from someone who doesn't actually know them. And he didn't know me—he knew the version of me I performed for him. The one carefully curated to avoid his wrath.

Eventually, when I got tired of performing, I started pushing back. Fighting more and more. On the surface, it looked like a conflict over curfews and rules.

But looking back now, I see it clearly. I wasn't fighting about the rules. I was fighting for myself.

We never really reconciled. As an adult, I worked on forgiveness and healing on my own, but true repair would have required him to see his role in our fractured relationship. And seeing that would have meant giving up control—something he couldn't do, even to his dying day.

As a parent of three adult children, I know things about their teenage years I sometimes wished I didn't. In some ways, control would've been the easier choice.

There were nights I lay awake wishing for ignorant bliss. Revelations that made my stomach drop and my mind race with worst-case scenarios.

One of those moments came when my son was nine or ten. I discovered he'd been exposed to pornography. He hadn't told me—I found out. My baby.

We thought we were safe parents. We thought we'd built the kind of relationship where he could tell us anything. But shame is powerful, and he carried it alone until I discovered what was happening.

My husband and I responded with care and didn't pile on shame or punishment, yet the shame he already felt had buried itself so deep that the struggle became darker than we could have imagined. There were days I didn't know if we'd find our way through.

But we did. We found the right help. We kept showing up, kept reassuring him he wasn't bad, and kept walking beside him through the darkness of his struggles. Slowly, we found the light together.

Parenting doesn't come with guarantees that your kids will tell you everything. But parenting in a way that creates the safest space for your kids to be themselves opens opportunities for your influence to remain—whether they tell you something or you find out.

My dad's control meant that when I struggled, I struggled alone. We chose influence, which meant that when our son struggled, we could walk through it with him. Not because we did everything right, but because the relationship could hold the weight of something this hard.

That's the difference between control and influence.

The Question Every Parent of a Teen Needs to Answer

If you're reading this, you probably have a tween or teen, which means you're standing at a crossroads. It's the moment when you have to decide: Do I want control, or do I want influence?

Because here's what I've learned after years of working with teenagers—first as a high school teacher, then as a mom, and now in the work I do with parents navigating these same years: You can't have both. And more importantly, control is a myth.

You can control a lot in your child's environment—routines, bedtimes, meals, and the shows they watch when they're little. But you can't actually control another human being. Of any age.

Remember when they were babies and you just wished that they would *sleep*? Out of your control. Toddlers melting down in the grocery store? Out of your control. And teenagers? Teenagers who want to do something will find a way. They have phones, friends with cars, bathroom windows, and a teenager's particular genius for creative problem-solving when properly motivated.

The real question isn't whether you can stop them from making mistakes—you can't, not completely. The question is whether you'll be someone they turn to when they do. Whether you'll have influence in their life when it really matters.

Building Influence Through Daily Connection

When my kids were entering their teen years, I was teaching high school and starting to worry: Was I getting too old to connect with teenagers?

But those years in the classroom taught me that connection isn't about being cool or young or having all the answers. It's about consistently showing up with genuine curiosity about their world, listening without immediately judging or jumping to conclusions, and seeing them as full human beings rather than problems to be solved or controlled.

That's what makes someone worth turning to when real problems arise—not permissiveness, but the knowledge that you'll actually listen. That you see them.

When the Hard Moment Comes

And the hard moment will come.

Maybe they'll tell you something you didn't want to know. Maybe you'll discover something they've been hiding. Maybe it'll be bigger than you expected, because truthfully, those moments are often just something you can't even imagine for your kid. I know this truth all too well.

All those small moments of connection—the genuine curiosity about their day, the times you bit your tongue and chose listening instead of lecturing—they're not just nice to have. They're essential building blocks in the foundation you'll need when things get hard.

Over my teaching years, students came to me with struggles they hadn't told their parents—pressure around sex, experiments with substances, friendship betrayals. "They'll freak out," they'd say. "They'll just punish me." These weren't bad parents. They'd prioritized control over connection, and now they were locked out—like my dad was.

This doesn't have to be your story. You don't have to be locked out. But it requires approaching things differently than your immediate impulses or traditional parenting advice might suggest.

Respond, Don't React: Three Things to Keep in Mind

When your teen tells you something difficult—or when you discover something they've been hiding—how you show up in the next few minutes can shape your relationship for the next few years.

1. Ground Yourself

Your initial facial expression and body language communicate volumes before you say a single word.

Your teen is watching you closely. They're measuring whether it's safe to be honest with you. If your face shows horror, disappointment, or anger, they're already shutting down. They're already deciding this was a mistake. They're already planning how to hide better next time.

Practice your "not shocked face" in advance. When they tell you something shocking, your face should communicate: "I can handle this. You're safe here. Keep talking."

Take a breath. Relax your shoulders. Keep your face neutral or gently concerned—not horrified.

This doesn't mean you approve. It doesn't mean you have no feelings. It means you're prioritizing connection over your initial emotional reaction.

2. Listen to Understand, Not to Respond

This is the hardest part for most parents. We want to fix, lecture, solve, or punish.

Stop. That's your control impulse talking. That's the voice that will shut down communication and lose you influence.

Instead, get genuinely curious. Your job right now isn't to solve this or teach a lesson. Your job is to understand what your teen is experiencing.

Try phrases like:

- "Tell me more about that."
- "Help me understand what this is like for you."
- "What led to this decision?"
- "How are you feeling about all of this?"

Listen fully. Don't interrupt with your opinions. Don't immediately correct their thinking. Just listen and try to see the situation through their eyes.

You might discover they're already feeling guilty. Maybe they're scared. Maybe they made a choice that seemed reasonable from their perspective, even if it looks obviously flawed from yours. Maybe they're in over their heads and desperately need help, but were afraid to ask.

You can't know any of this if you're too busy reacting to really listen.

3. Offer Support and Guidance

Here's where you get to decide what you really want your teen to learn from this experience.

Do you want them to learn resilience? That they're capable of navigating hard things? That mistakes don't define them? That you're a safe person to turn to when life gets complicated?

Or do you want them to learn shame? That they should hide their struggles better next time? That your love and support are conditional on their perfect behavior?

Your response determines which lessons they learn. Read that again.

This doesn't mean there is no accountability. Natural consequences exist. Better still are solutions you build alongside them that teach how to do better next time. These responses build character and problem-solving skills. Punishment and consequences that aim to control build resentment and disconnection.

Instead of "I'm taking your phone for a month," try: "I can see this situation is complicated, and I'm glad you told me. I need some time to think about how we handle this together. What I know for sure right now is that I love you, and we're going to figure this out."

Ask questions like:

- "What do you think needs to happen now?"
- "How can I support you in making this right?"

You're teaching them that mistakes don't end the relationship. You're teaching them that honesty is met with partnership, not punishment. You're building influence that will matter when the next hard thing comes—because there will be a next hard thing.

Why This Matters More Than You May Think

My dad never had these conversations with me because his need for control never gave me the chance.

Control doesn't prevent mistakes—it just means you don't know about them. It means your teen navigates them alone, without your guidance, without your support.

Choosing influence means living with more uncertainty than control promises. It means there will be nights you lie awake wishing you didn't know what you know.

But what you gain is worth infinitely more.

You gain a relationship with the real person your teen is becoming. You gain the ability to guide them when it matters. You gain their trust that you can handle their real life. You gain the opportunity to walk through hard things together. And you gain a deeply connected, lifelong relationship with them.

If you realize you've been choosing control, it's not too late. You might even say: "I've been thinking about how I respond when you tell me hard things, and I realize I haven't always made it easy for you to be honest with me. I want to change that. I want to be someone you can talk to, even when—especially when—things are messy or complicated."

Your teen is standing at the threshold of their room right now, deciding whether to close the door or invite you in. And this is your moment to choose as well—control or influence.

Choose wisely.

Melanie Zwyghuizen is the founder of Gen 1 Parenting, a nonprofit making parenting education accessible to every caregiver. With over 30 years of teaching high school, raising three children, and coaching hundreds of families, she specializes in helping parents navigate the teen years with confidence and connection. A Certified Parent Educator and Coach with a Master of Education, Melanie offers practical, relational strategies grounded in real life. When she's not supporting families, she enjoys spending time with her family, walking, reading, and relaxing on the shores of Lake Michigan. Scan the QR code for your free in-depth guide, Ground Yourself, Not Your Teen, and learn more at gen1parenting.org

FROM TANTRUMS TO TEEN YEARS: WHY CONNECTION STILL COMES FIRST

Susan B. Carroll, M.Ed.

———

"If my child is like this at age two, I'm afraid of what the teen years will be like!"

I hear this a lot from the families in my preschool. When their toddler or preschooler is acting, well, like a toddler or preschooler, and exhibiting behavior that the parent does not enjoy, they jump to the worst-case scenario: an upset teenager will be like a toddler tantrum, but a thousand times harder. The teen years become something to fear—rude, door-slamming, parent-hating people—because that's the story we've been told. So parents do everything in their power to squash difficult behavior now, hoping it will make the teen years smoother. Yet when asked, most parents don't actually want compliant children. They want a happy, connected home with their future teens. Is that possible? As a mom of two teenagers and a young adult, I'm here to assure you it is. However, to tame teen-year fears, we need to understand and accept teens for who they are.

Understanding Your Child's Development

Did you know your teenager's brain is growing almost as quickly as it did as a baby and toddler? As an early childhood educator and preschool director, I know how crucial those first five years of life are for our children. This is a time of amazing and rapid brain development. What many parents are unaware of is that during adolescence, our children's brains go through a second period of significant growth that begins in adolescence and ends when our child is about 25 years old.

The last part of the brain to develop is your teen's prefrontal cortex, which is the reasoning center of the brain. In other words, the part of our brains that helps us plan, make decisions, regulate our emotions, and have self-control is the last part to develop. Add to this the fact that teens are also marinating in hormones and self-doubt, and you can see why it may be hard for your teenager to get along with everyone else in the family.

Along with this rapid brain development, your teen's emotional landscape is changing as well. Similar to when they were younger, they are still grappling with how to identify and express their emotions. Hormonal changes and a new awareness of how they fit into society's fabric play a big role in this as well. Teenagers become hyper-aware of their peers and are heavily influenced by them. Societal pressures to fit in can also lead teens to feel increasingly self-conscious and anxious. All of these factors contribute to a lot of emotional upheaval for your teenager. No wonder so many parents dread the teen years.

While all of this development and emotional disequilibrium is happening, your teenager is shifting their time and attention away from you and toward their peers. Social connection with their friends becomes central to a teen's life and highly influences their behavior. This is why it is crucial we build and maintain our relationship with our teens during this time in their lives.

Building and Maintaining a Relationship with Your Teen

Remember when your toddler had tantrums? How did you handle it? Did you yell back at them? Send them to their room?

I recommend emotion coaching to the parents I work with. Following John Gottman's approach, parents are encouraged to recognize and validate their children's feelings.[1] They listen with empathy, help children name their feelings, and support problem-solving. When our children are young, this feels easier. We comfort them and say, "I see you are disappointed and upset." We help them find a solution, if possible, and allow them to have their feelings without judgment or shame. Yet we often do not provide this same nurturing to our teens.

We expect so much of teenagers because they present as almost-adults, and in many ways, they are. However, teens are their own special creatures with emerging skills, complicated emotions, and a desire to be accepted and loved. This need for love and acceptance is key to our relationship with our teens.

Dan Siegel often says we need to connect before we correct our child's behavior.[2] The reason is quite simple: when we connect with our child emotionally, it allows them to trust us, which in turn makes discipline possible. Correction without connection creates conflict.

Connection is Key

From the time our children are first born, their attachment to their caregiver is the most important bond they can develop. This remains true as our children grow. In fact, I would argue that teenagers need even more connection time than young children do, as teens are navigating big emotions, life pressures, and finding who they are in the world.

Whenever there is an uptick in challenging behavior, I ask parents I work with if they have been doing special time with their child. The answer is usually no. I give them an assignment: spend 20 minutes of special time with your child each day for the next week, and then report back to me. Without fail, the parents come back the next week and tell me their child's behavior has improved. That is how simple special time is. Nothing else has changed in the home, so it almost seems like a magical fix. However, the reason it works so well is that your child is craving your attention and has now received it on a consistent basis.

Here's what makes special time work: it's one-on-one, phone away, no multitasking. Your child chooses the activity. It doesn't require leaving the house or spending money, and it's not the time for homework or piano practice. The only rule is that it's fun, safe, and screen-free.

You may wonder how special time works with teenagers—no more blocks and cars on the floor. That depends on your teenager. Special time is an incredible opportunity to show your teen that you are interested in the things that are important to them. Maybe it is listening to music together, playing a board game, creating art, or building something together. Special time may be as simple as listening to their interests. Can you name which bands they listen to or which shows they watch? Make the time to find out what interests and excites them.

Connecting with your teen means connecting with their friends as well. Not in a "I'm so cool and part of your group" kind of way, but in a genuine way of showing care to the friends in their lives. Our house is the place my teenagers' friends like to hang out. There is nothing fancy or elaborate about our place; in fact, it is a small, modest home, but the teens are happy to pile into our family room and watch movies, play games, sing karaoke, or just hang out. The reason is that we treat all of them with respect, know their names, and show that we care about them. We also provide a lot of snacks.

While connection is paramount in our relationship with our teens, that alone will not prevent them from making mistakes or from needing our guidance. So, what do we do when our children act out or otherwise make poor decisions?

Teaching Your Teen

What does the word discipline mean to you? Does it mean consequences? Ultimatums? Conflict?

Did you know that the word discipline actually means "to teach"? How could it look in your home if you approached your teen as a teacher rather than an enforcer?

Discipline teaches children to handle emotions, understand cause and effect, internalize decision-making, and it includes setting limits. Through discipline, we encourage desired behaviors, prevent misbehavior, connect with our children, and resolve problem behavior. We do this by observing what is happening with our child and asking, "What does my child need? What do I need to teach them?" Knowing what our children need takes patience and sometimes a little detective work. If your teenager is acting sullen or angry, try to figure out why. Remember that behavior is a form of communication of an unmet need.[3] What is your child's behavior trying to tell you? Once you have discovered the meaning behind your teen's behavior, you can begin to work with them to find a solution to the problem.

An important facet of discipline is that it does not need to be imposed from the outside. It is something we create, figure out, and modify with our children. This comes from creating and fostering a strong relationship with our children where they know they are valued, respected, and included. However, this does not mean that children are in charge or have an equal say in all decisions. Remember, their brains are still growing, so you will need to give their frontal lobes a lot of support. What this approach does is respect the child and treat them as an active participant in their own development. They will learn more and push back less when you work with them rather than against them.

Not Your Friend, Still Your Person

Your teen is not your enemy, but they are not your friend either. Even though they present as adult-like, they still need a parent/caregiver to guide and support them. Teenagers are hilarious, sweet, misunderstood young people. I don't always understand what my teens are talking about, but that doesn't mean what they are saying isn't valuable. They are straddling the space between childhood and adulthood, which leaves them feeling anxious and uncertain. Their coping mechanism may be to lash out at you. Remember that they do this with the people they feel most comfortable with, and you are doing a great job as a parent if that person is you. Your job is to continue to create a safe, reliable environment for your teen that has consistent boundaries and a lot of love.

When your teen sees you as someone they trust, they will continue to come to you with their problems, ask for advice, and share their emotions with you. They will also be more open to your guidance and correction. As you work with your child, rather than against them, you will find the teen years can be an amazing experience for both you and your child. After all, this is a time to see the wonderful person your child is *right* now, and get a glimpse into the adult they will soon become.

Susan B. Carroll is a Parent Educator and Director of a cooperative preschool program in Washington State. She holds a master's degree in education from the University of Washington and a BA from Loyola University, Chicago. For over twenty years, Susan has taught at the preschool and elementary school levels, as well as spending the past ten years working in higher education. Susan is passionate about working with families to help them develop the foundational skills they need to be the best parents for their children. Join Susan's "Parenting Playground" for parenting advice and support for children of all ages at https://www.parenting-playground.com/

THE ADOLESCENT BRAIN: UNDER CONSTRUCTION

Jean M. Clinton, MD

Adolescence often feels like unfamiliar territory for parents. Children who were once affectionate, eager to please, and predictable may suddenly seem emotionally intense, impulsive, private, or distant.

Parents often ask, "What happened?" or "Did I do something wrong?" These questions are not signs of failure. They are signs of care, and they reflect how deeply invested parents are in their children's well-being.

Over the past several decades, advances in neuroscience have fundamentally changed how we understand adolescence. We now know that many of the behaviors that concern parents during the teen years are not evidence of poor character or deliberate opposition. Rather, they reflect a brain that is still developing. Adolescence is not a detour from healthy development, nor a problem to be fixed. It is a critical period of brain reorganization, emotional growth, social learning, and possibility.

Understanding what is happening in the adolescent brain does not make parenting effortless, but it does make it more compassionate. When parents can view behavior through a developmental lens, they are better able to respond with curiosity rather than fear, and with connection rather than control. This shift in perspective can transform everyday interactions and reduce conflict during a time that often feels demanding for families.

Brains Under Construction

One of the most important discoveries in developmental neuroscience is that the human brain continues to mature well beyond childhood. Brain imaging studies show that development continues into the mid-twenties, with different systems maturing at different rates. The areas of the brain responsible for planning, impulse control, emotional regulation, and anticipating consequences are among the last to fully develop.

At the same time, emotional and reward systems become highly active during adolescence. These systems are sensitive to novelty, excitement, and social reward. This developmental timing creates a mismatch that many parents recognize immediately: strong emotions and powerful motivations paired with still-developing self-control.

Some researchers describe this as having a fast accelerator with brakes that are still under construction.

This mismatch does not mean that adolescents are incapable of thinking or reasoning. Teens often demonstrate sophisticated insight, creativity, and moral reasoning, particularly in calm situations.

However, in emotionally charged moments or in the presence of peers, the systems responsible for reflection and inhibition are less available. What appears to be poor judgment is often a reflection of developmental timing rather than a lack of values or understanding.

Another key concept is neuroplasticity—the brain's ability to change in response to experience. During adolescence, the brain is especially responsive to what it repeatedly encounters. Neural connections that are used frequently become stronger, while those that are used less often are pruned away. This process helps the brain become more efficient, but it also means that experiences during adolescence have a lasting impact.

Relationships, stress, learning environments, and repeated emotional experiences all shape the development of neural pathways. This is why adolescence is a period of both vulnerability and opportunity.

Supportive experiences strengthen circuits related to regulation, empathy, and resilience, while chronic stress or disconnection can make development more difficult.

Emotion, Behavior, and Meaning

A helpful starting point for parents is the reminder that all behavior has a reason and happens in a context. Adolescents are not trying to be difficult on purpose. When teens are not doing well, it usually reflects unmet needs, stress, or developing skills.

Adolescents experience emotions more intensely than adults. Brain imaging research shows that teens rely more heavily on fast-acting emotional systems when interpreting situations, particularly facial expressions and tone of voice. As a result, they may read more anger, threat, or rejection into adult expressions than is intended. This can lead to misunderstandings and conflict, even in well-functioning families.

Because emotional systems develop earlier than regulatory systems, teens may feel deeply before they can explain what they are feeling. This can look like overreaction, withdrawal, or sudden mood shifts.

Calm, predictable adult responses help adolescents learn to regulate themselves. When adults remain grounded, they lend their nervous systems to young people whose own systems are still under construction.

Risk-taking is another visible feature of adolescence. Reward systems are highly sensitive during this period, making the potential payoff of an experience—excitement, belonging, approval—feel especially powerful. Teens are often aware of risks, but emotional and social rewards can outweigh long-term considerations, particularly in peer settings.

Peers, Belonging, and Social Worlds

Peer relationships take on heightened importance during adolescence for good developmental reasons. Humans are biologically wired to seek peer connection during this stage as part of learning independence, cooperation, and social identity. Adolescents are not rejecting their parents when peers matter more; they are following a developmental pathway that supports growth.

Belonging is a powerful driver of behavior during adolescence. Feeling excluded, shamed, or disconnected can be deeply distressing for a developing brain. Conversely, feeling accepted and valued supports emotional regulation and resilience. Parents who remain curious about their teen's social world—without interrogating or dismissing it—help create a bridge between home and peer life.

Research consistently shows that relationships with caring adults remain protective throughout adolescence. Teens with strong adult connections are better able to navigate peer pressure, recover from stress, and seek help when they need it. Parents continue to matter deeply, even when adolescents act as though they do not.

Stress, Sleep, and Vulnerability

Adolescence is also a time when stress can have a significant impact on mental health. Because systems involved in stress regulation are still developing, adolescents are often more sensitive to pressure than adults realize. Academic expectations, social comparison, uncertainty about the future, and exposure to distressing news or online content can all activate stress responses that feel overwhelming.

When stress is chronic or feels unmanageable, it can interfere with attention, mood, sleep, and behavior. What may look like laziness, irritability, or disengagement is often a nervous system doing its best to cope. Supportive relationships play a central role in helping adolescents manage stress.

Feeling emotionally safe with adults changes how the brain processes challenge and adversity.

Sleep is another critical factor in adolescent well-being. Teen circadian rhythms naturally shift later, even though adolescents need more sleep than adults. Chronic sleep deprivation affects mood, learning, and behavior, and can intensify emotional reactivity. Understanding the biological basis of teen sleep patterns can help parents approach this issue with empathy rather than frustration.

Substances such as alcohol and marijuana can interfere with brain development, particularly when use begins early and is frequent. Conversations about substance use are most effective when grounded in relationship, curiosity, and accurate information rather than fear or punishment.

Why Parents Still Matter

One of the most persistent myths about adolescence is that teenagers no longer need their parents. Brain science tells us the opposite. Adolescents continue to need emotionally available, consistent adults who offer safety, guidance, and reassurance—even when teens push away or appear indifferent.

Parents do not need to be perfect. What matters most is presence. Teens benefit from adults whose eyes light up when they enter the room, who set clear boundaries with warmth, and who remain connected even during conflict. Repair after rupture is especially powerful. When parents acknowledge mistakes and reconnect, they model accountability and resilience.

A developmental lens invites parents to shift from asking, "How do I stop this behavior?" to "What is my teen learning right now?" This reframing does not remove the need for boundaries, but it grounds them in guidance rather than fear.

Adolescence as a Period of Promise

Adolescence is a time of enormous potential. With supportive relationships, meaningful activities, and understanding adults, teenage brains develop in ways that support resilience, empathy, creativity, and long-term well-being. Growth during this period is rarely linear. There are steps forward and steps back, particularly during periods of rapid change.

Holding a long view can be challenging when behavior feels intense or concerning. Yet development unfolds over time, shaped by experience and relationship. Adolescence is not simply something to survive. It is a window during which brains are being built in response to how young people are treated and understood.

Love builds brains—including teenage brains. The relationship parents have with their adolescents remains one of the most powerful influences in their lives, even when it feels strained or uncertain.

Presence, patience, and connection matter more than parents may realize.

Dr. Jean M. Clinton, a McMaster University graduate with a Bachelor of Music (Honours) and Doctor of Medicine, is a Clinical Professor at McMaster University and a renowned child psychiatrist whose work has profoundly influenced the understanding of relationships, brain development, and mental well-being. A Fellow of the ZERO TO THREE Academy, she has served as an Education Advisor to the Premier and Minister of Education for Ontario and on multiple national and international advisory bodies, including UNICEF Canada and the Canadian Pediatric Society. Author of *Love Builds Brains* and co-author of *Ontario: A Learning Province*, Dr. Clinton's teaching and scholarship bridge neuroscience, education, and deep learning in child development.

WHAT YOUR TEEN REALLY NEEDS TO BUILD EMOTIONAL RESILIENCE

Dr. Kirstin Barchia, Clinical Psychologist, PhD, MClinPsych, BPsych(Hons)

I cried when I received the text.

It was from a parent I had been working with. She wanted to know what to do.

Her teen had just told her she wanted to kill herself.

I cried when I read the text, but not for the reason you may think.

It was because everything I had been working on with this family had led to this life-saving moment. The moment when this teen needed the safety net of her family, she was able to use it.

In my work as a Clinical Psychologist, I have had hundreds of parents sit in front of me desperately wanting to learn the secret to building an emotionally resilient teen. Parents are often surprised by my answer. They expect me to talk about sleep, social media, screen time, boundaries, mindfulness, breathing, diet, or exercise. And while these things are important, they're not the only things you as a parent can provide your teen.

Your relationship with your teen is key to their resilience.

Research has shown that a connected parent-teen relationship is protective, not just in moments of crisis, but it's linked to lower rates of teen mental health, behavioral, attention, and concentration problems, better teen coping and social skills, less conflict with peers, and less drinking, drug use, and other risky behaviors.

There's a common misunderstanding that resilience is the same as grit. Such that trekking through the woods alone in the rain proves you're resilient. This leads many parents to worry when their teen struggles to unpack a dishwasher at the end of the day, let alone attend a school camp in the actual woods. But resilience is much more than internal personal characteristics or grit. Resilience is also a person's ability to access support to overcome a challenge.

This generation of teens is facing more challenges than any previous generation. Rates of mental health struggles and suicide are higher than they have ever been. Now more than ever, we need to build support for teens.

The teen sitting alone in their room after being excluded from a group chat needs a parent to talk to at 11 p.m. The teen who is terrified to go to school needs a parent they can talk to at 7 a.m. The teen who has thoughts of suicide or self-harm needs a parent they can tell at any time of the day. Being an emotional support for your teen does not make them weak; when done right, it builds their resilience.

Your teen needs to be able to talk to you.

And while you might be reading this thinking, *Of course, my teen can talk to me about anything. I always tell them they can talk to me.* Teens look to other cues to decide whether they can actually talk to their parents about their tough feelings.

Why is the parent-teen relationship so important to resilience? I'll give you three reasons.

1. How you respond creates their template.

On my walk to work each day, I pass a children's playground. I've had many opportunities to watch parents respond when a toddler falls and hurts themselves. Parents vary in how they respond. Some pick up the toddler in frustration at their constant crying and leave the park. Some ignore the tears or tell them they're big and strong and don't need to cry. And others pick up the child, comfort them, and help them get back into play. Each of these responses teaches a different lesson: that emotions are too much, that feelings should be hidden, or that feelings pass and help is available.

Well before the teen years, your teen was watching how you responded to emotions. And they are still watching (and testing) you every day. Their willingness to reach out for help from you (and others) comes from repeated experiences in the small and big moments of life that teach them that no feeling is too big, that you can be there for them, and that feelings pass.

As emotions grow in the teen years, there's a second window for your teen to learn how you will respond. Your reactions when they yell at you and tell you they're too tired to unload the dishwasher, or when they slam their door and tell you that you don't understand how hard their life is, or when they tell you they hate school—these show them how you handle their bigger feelings now.

Many parents, understandably, see these moments of refusal and rudeness as signs that they need to discipline their teen. But often, what underlies the refusal to unload the dishwasher or the swearing under their breath as they slam the door is an emotionally overwhelmed teen rather than a defiant one.

In the same way that the child on the playground responds to parental emotional support and can return to play, when parents look underneath the behavior to acknowledge and support their teen's emotions, teens can often calm down, and even apologize for bad language without you having to tell them—all the while learning that you are a safe and helpful person to share feelings with.

2. What you say becomes their inner voice.

On my morning walk, I used to walk past a school gate. On the sidewalk were encouraging words to students that read, "Reach for the stars!" "You're awesome just the way you are!" "Only you can be you, so just be you!" Many parents try their best to feed their children encouragement and positivity because they know how important it is. On good days, this isn't too hard.

But when your teen swears at you and calls you a terrible parent, when they've hurt their sibling and won't apologize, when they've lost a sock and are late for school, or when your kitchen has no cups because they're all in their room, it's hard not to get frustrated and call them lazy, selfish, mean, or disorganized, or yell, "What's wrong with you!"

But what you say to your teen about their character in these moments matters. It can be hard sometimes to see the impact of your words on your teen when they seem not to listen, throw in their earbuds, or shrug and walk away. But what you say counts. Not just for today, but for their whole lives. We all carry our parents' words with us for the rest of our lives. Think about it for a minute. You can probably still hear your parents' voices in your head, whether you like it or not.

That time you yelled, "What's wrong with you?" It sticks. And can come out later in life as an anxiety that deep down "there's something wrong with me." I've worked with many adults in therapy who struggle with motivation and depression because they believe they're lazy and that there's something wrong with them. The words you use when you respond to your teen's difficulties either create or reinforce negative thoughts about themselves, or they speak internal strength and resilience into their lives—not just for today but for the future.

But before you start to worry about the damage you or your partner may have done, know this: you can help with the repair. You can't be perfect. And it would feel weird and robotic if you were always sunshine and words of positivity with your teen. Your teen doesn't need perpetual positivity; they need understanding. If you now understand your teen differently and regret things you have said to them, share your new understanding with them.

So next time your teen does something upsetting, it's okay to resist fears about them having poor character and decide instead to see the good person underneath. You have a good kid: they just struggle at times. You don't have to change their character. Underneath, they're good. And fostering that belief is an important part of their lifelong emotional resilience.

Helping them change behaviors that hurt others or undermine their resilience is still important, but not because they have a flawed character. Your relationship with them is the foundation upon which you can help them change.

3. Your conversations can help them change.

When teens are fighting to stay up late, want more screen time, won't eat healthy, or won't exercise, parents are left scratching their heads, wondering what they can do to help their teen make better decisions about their health and well-being. But before you threaten to unplug Wi-Fi again, or give up and resign yourself to sitting back and watching them make bad decisions, your relationship can be the foundation for conversations that lead to real behavior change.

While parents often spend a lot of time trying to learn the magic thing to say to get them to change, no matter how well-meaning your wonderful, knowledgeable insights are, your teen will likely roll their eyes and tune out if they're delivered in the wrong way.

Teens need help changing their own behavior, but not by telling them what to do. In the same way you wouldn't jump in to answer the question on your teen's math homework, you need to resist the temptation to jump in with the "answers" to their life problems. Instead of telling your teen what to do about screen use, sleep, or their latest friendship difficulty, ask them questions to help them think through how they want to approach the problem. Approaching it this way teaches them the thinking skills they need to work through problems, take responsibility, motivate themselves, and change their own behaviors. The solutions they generate are also more likely to be successful because, often, as parents, we don't have all the information about the problem. And here's what often happens: after you've listened and asked questions, your teen turns to you and asks for your advice. When they ask, they actually listen—because you listened first.

Tonight, when your teen speaks rudely at the table, doesn't want to unpack the dishwasher, or stomps off and slams a door, try this: be curious about what's happening underneath, resist the temptation to judge, fix, or react immediately. Remember how you respond in these moments forms the foundation of their internal dialogue and their sense of whether you are willing to understand them, be there for them, and help them with the frustrations of life. You can always circle back to a productive conversation about chores or communication later, but first respond to the emotions underneath. It's these moments that build or break connection and are the beginning of building the emotional resilience you want for them. Your relationship with your teen is not just a "nice to have." It's something they want and need, both now and in the future.

Dr. Kirstin Barchia, PhD, MClinPsych, is a Clinical Psychologist with 25 years of experience working with parents of teenagers. She watched great parents unknowingly make mistakes—not from a lack of effort, but from a lack of support. When she searched for resources, she found vague advice like "connect with your teen" without practical strategies. So she created the Calm Connection program, grounded in her research on adolescent behavior and resilience. Access her free resource to improve calm and connection in your family—and reduce the eye rolls, moodiness, and closed doors—at www.kirstinbarchia.com.au/connection.

WHEN THE OLD TOOLS STOP WORKING

Raquel Santos Miñarro

———

I did not realize I had crossed into parenting a teenager until I was already in it.

There was no clear line, no announcement, no moment I could point to and say, "This is different now." It happened quietly, through small ruptures: conversations that no longer landed, limits that suddenly felt intrusive, emotions that escalated faster than I could follow.

For a long time, I thought the problem was communication.

I tried to explain myself better. I used more words, clearer words, calmer words. I repeated myself. I softened my tone. I justified my decisions. I believed that if I could just say things the right way, she would understand.

What I did not see at first was that I was still speaking from a place that belonged to childhood, a place where authority worked, where explanations were enough, where obedience felt natural.

It was the language many of us grew up with: a framework shaped by generations in which adults led, and children followed, where being under someone's care meant being under their command.

But the world has changed. And so have our children.

What they ask from us now is not obedience, but relationship. Not control, but connection.

My teen was not rejecting my words. She was rejecting the position I was speaking from.

The real shift came after a big argument, the kind that leaves everyone shaken and quiet afterward.

Later that day, I found a note she had left for me. She does that sometimes. I keep them all.

In it, she wrote that she felt unseen. That something in our dynamic no longer felt right to her. That I needed to understand how things worked now. She was clear about what she needed from me: space, respect, and a different kind of presence.

She told me I could not control her. Not now, not ever. What she was trying to express was that obedience was no longer the framework she lived in.

I read the note slowly. And to my own surprise, it did not hurt. It felt honest. Clear. Brave.

What she was really saying was: *Mom, I am growing. I need space to decide. I need you to see me differently.*

That note marked something important for me, not because she was setting a boundary, but because I realized I had to change more than she did.

Until then, I had been focused on managing her emotions, her reactions, her choices. I had not fully realized how much of the work ahead belonged to me.

I knew the theory. I had taught it. I facilitated workshops, led parent conversations, and spoke about communication, emotional regulation, limits, and autonomy.

And still, nothing prepared me for how difficult it is to apply all of that when the person standing in front of you is your own child.

Because the theory assumes calm. Real life comes with fear. Fear that they will fail. Fear that they will not be enough. Fear that if we do not intervene now, we are somehow failing them — and ourselves.

That is the part we do not talk about enough.

Most parents do not control because they want power. They control because they are scared: scared of being judged by other adults, by teachers, family members, or other parents; scared of the consequences their children might face if they make the wrong choice, fall behind, or get hurt; and, above all, scared of watching them struggle and feeling helpless in the process.

When fear takes the lead, urgency follows. We feel responsible for preventing every mistake, every discomfort, every possible outcome. So we explain more than necessary. We correct quickly. We insist. We step in too fast.

Not because we do not trust our children, but because we do not trust what will happen if we do not intervene, but because sitting with that uncertainty can feel unbearable.

One of the hardest shifts for me was learning when not to speak. Not the kind of silence that disengages or withdraws, but the kind that stays present without taking over. The silence where you see them making a choice you would not make. Where you can already predict the outcome. Where every cell in your body wants to intervene. And you do not.

Instead, you stay. You breathe. You regulate yourself. Not because you agree, but because you are choosing relationship over control.

This kind of silence feels unbearable at first. From the outside, it can look like inaction. Inside, it is work: holding your tongue, holding your fear, holding the urge to fix, and holding the relationship steady while your teen experiences the consequences of their choices. Because our role is not to prevent pain, but to prevent loneliness.

This stage of parenting demands something no one prepared us for. It asks us to grieve: the child who needed us differently, the authority that once worked, the illusion that doing everything "right" would guarantee an easy path.

At the same time, it asks us to grow. To relate differently. To guide instead of control. To listen instead of fix. To respond instead of react.

None of this happens through intellectual understanding alone. It happens in real time, through experience, missteps, and repetition.

There are moments when I notice myself moving toward control instead of connection. Moments when fear takes the lead, when I react before I regulate. When that happens, repair becomes necessary. And learning to repair is part of the work. Because none of us is doing this perfectly; not us as parents, not them as teens, not as human beings.

What matters is not getting it right every time, but being willing to notice, return, and reconnect when we miss the mark.

This is what that shift looks like in real life: moments that feel small, yet carry everything we are learning.

My teen chooses to handle a disagreement with a friend independently. I can already anticipate how it might go wrong. My first impulse is to step in, to guide the conversation, to protect from the fallout. Instead, I pause. I breathe. I stay present, reminding myself that I am available if I am truly needed, not simply when discomfort arises.

Another day, my teen forgets something important. The consequence is minor, but unpleasant. The familiar urge to rescue or explain appears. This time, I choose not to intervene and allow the experience to unfold.

Sometimes it is losing things. Sometimes it is leaving schoolwork until the last minute.

Each time I rush in to manage what is not mine to manage, I delay the very capacity I hope to foster.

These moments make the inner work visible. Not because I always get it right — I do not — but because I notice myself choosing differently.

Less control. More presence. Less fear-driven reaction. More trust in the process.

This shift has not been easy. Resisting the urge to fix, tolerating discomfort, and staying regulated when emotions rise require constant attention. There is also the quiet shame that can surface when teens struggle; the feeling that their mistakes somehow reflect our failure as parents.

And yet, there are moments when I manage to pause instead of react, to listen without correcting, to hold limits without controlling.

They may seem small, but they change the tone of the relationship. They create space for learning rather than fear.

This work does not look the same in every family. Some teens push back loudly, others withdraw. Some need space; others need reassurance. The approach adapts, but the need for connection remains.

Parenting teens is not about mastering techniques or finding the perfect words. It is about shifting how we show up — noticing our fear, learning to regulate ourselves, and staying emotionally available as they begin to navigate life on their own.

The insight that changed everything for me is simple, but not easy to accept: the most powerful way to guide a teen is to first hold yourself.

From there, other things begin to follow. Respect feels less forced. Autonomy becomes less threatening. Responsibility stops being something to demand and becomes something that can grow. Connection does not disappear. It changes.

This kind of inner work does not come from knowing more. It comes from practice — from noticing our triggers, pausing when everything urges us to react, and choosing, again and again, to respond differently.

The journey is never perfect. We fail. We repair. We try again.

I thought I was losing control. I was learning how to stay with what was happening, rather than trying to control what came next.

Raquel Santos Miñarro, M.Sc., M.A.Ed., is a Certified Positive Discipline Parent Educator based on Spain's Mediterranean coast after living fifteen years in California. With a professional path in education spanning over two decades, she has supported parents and educators since 2020 in strengthening communication, emotional regulation, and respectful relationships with teens. Raising her own children became a turning point that reshaped how she understands and supports families, alongside her years of teaching and work in education, shaping a practical and reflective approach. You can get in touch with her at rsantosminarro@gmail.com

6

CLOSE ENOUGH TO MATTER: BUILDING CONNECTION WITH YOUR ADOLESCENT

Amélie Friedrich

I was walking with my son through the woods near our home when he turned to me and said, unprompted, "I love you." It was the first time he had ever said it spontaneously. In that moment, the autumn leaves crunching beneath our feet, I knew I was finally on the right track.

When I became a parent, I did not have the knowledge about what every parent and child needs in order to thrive—even though I was a psychologist. My training had taught me about child development and behavior, but somehow the practical wisdom of building deep connection had eluded me. It took me several years to learn this. I must say that during those early years, parenthood was not particularly enjoyable for me. There were more power struggles than peaceful moments, more frustration than fulfillment. I wish I had known then what I learned later, because those precious years will not come back.

My son is a teenager now, and he still says and shows me he loves me. He seeks me out to talk about his day, shares his worries and his triumphs, and genuinely enjoys spending time together. What made the difference? One critical piece of the parenting puzzle: the relationship I built with him. That relationship did not happen by accident—it required intention, consistency, and a willingness to change my approach.

Of course, building that relationship is not always easy. Rolling eyes, slamming doors, rude remarks, dismissive sighs—the behaviors adolescents can display make it quite easy for parents to feel distant from their child. But the reactions of many parents also create distance in return. When we respond to rudeness with harshness, we widen the gap instead of bridging it. The good news is that connection can be strengthened at any time. It is never too late to start.

Why Your Relationship Matters More Than Ever

Having a strong relationship with at least one primary caregiver is a crucial protective factor for a child's mental health—and it is also a parent's most powerful tool when it comes to guiding behavior. In a world full of influences competing for your teenager's attention and allegiance, your relationship is what keeps you in the conversation.

Research consistently shows that children's mental health is highly influenced by the quality of their relationships with their parents. A positive parent-child relationship makes children more resilient when facing life's challenges—whether those challenges involve academic pressure, social difficulties, or the inevitable heartbreaks of growing up. Furthermore, contemporary parenting experts agree that when you have a good relationship with your child, you have more influence on their behavior—they are more likely to listen to your guidance and do what you ask.

The reason is simple: people are more likely to do things for people they like and feel connected to. A request from someone we feel disconnected from will probably be met with resistance. Think about your own life—when a boss you respect asks you to take on extra work, you are far more willing than when a boss who has treated you poorly makes the same request. The reality is that we ask our children to do many things they do not especially want to do—cleaning their rooms, doing homework, getting off their devices—and we do this daily. When your child feels connected to you, living together becomes less frustrating and more enjoyable for everyone.

This influence matters especially during adolescence, when teens are often drawn to risky behavior—alcohol, tobacco, drugs, dangerous driving, unhealthy relationships. The stakes are higher than when they were younger. A wrong decision at fifteen can have consequences that last a lifetime. You do not want to lose your influence at the very time it is most needed.

Emotional health. Positive behavior. Resilience. These are the gifts of connection. This is not just any relationship—it is one of the most precious and critical relationships your child will ever have. The foundation you build now will support them for decades to come.

Take a moment now to reflect on your relationship with your child. Do you have many friendly interactions, or are most interactions stressful? Are there moments of genuine warmth and laughter, or does it feel like you are always correcting, directing, or arguing? How would you describe the relationship in a few words? If there is room for improvement, read on. The tools are simpler than you might think.

Building and Strengthening Connection

So how do we create a good relationship—or strengthen the one we already have? A child feels close to their parent when the parent communicates respectfully, soothes them when they struggle, tries to understand them, and spends enjoyable time with them. These four pillars of connection work together to create a relationship that can weather the storms of adolescence. Let us look at each of these in turn.

Communication: Words and Beyond

The way we speak to our children directly affects whether they feel close to us or distant. Respectful communication builds connection; criticism and harsh discipline erode it. Every interaction is either a deposit into the relationship bank account or a withdrawal from it.

Think about how you communicate with your friends, colleagues, and other adults. Do you speak to your child with the same respect? You probably do not yell at your friends when they forget something. You do not say to your partner, "If you don't take out the garbage this morning, I'll take your phone away for today." Imagine someone speaking to you that way—how would you feel about that person? Would you feel motivated to help them? Would you want to spend time with them? Most likely not.

Parents often believe that because they are the parents, their children should respect them no matter what. But if you are not respectful toward your children, do not expect respect in return. Respect must be mutual, even when parents are in charge. Respectful communication means no yelling, no threatening, no blaming, no name-calling—and no punishing. If most of your interactions involve complaining, criticizing, and demanding, that will definitely impact your relationship. Your child will begin to avoid you, hide things from you, and tune out your voice.

I want to emphasize that there are better ways to guide behavior, but the relationship must come first. Children absolutely need at least one supportive adult during the bumpy ride of adolescence—someone they can turn to when things get hard. Punishment damages your relationship and undermines your ability to be that person for your child. When they face a crisis, will they come to you or hide from you?

Of course, even knowing this, we adults will sometimes yell or say things we regret. We all do—that is part of being human. The goal is not perfection but consistency. Most of the time, we aim for calm and respectful. And when ruptures happen, we repair them. This might sound like: "I shouldn't have yelled at you. I was frustrated, but that's no excuse. I'm sorry." Modeling how to take responsibility and make amends teaches your child a valuable life skill.

One more thing about communication: staying connected requires you to be regulated yourself. If you are depleted—exhausted, stressed, overwhelmed—you will snap. And snapping ruptures the relationship.

Taking care of yourself is taking care of your relationship with your child. This is not selfishness; it is wisdom.

Beyond words, nonverbal communication matters deeply. A soft tone of voice, a relaxed facial expression, an open posture—these signals tell your child you are safe, not threatening. Physical affection matters too: a hug, a hand on their shoulder, a warm smile, a kiss goodnight, a wink across the dinner table. And perhaps most importantly, let your eyes light up when you see them after being apart. That moment of visible delight communicates volumes. Hugging releases oxytocin, the hormone that bonds people to each other. Often communicate to your child—verbally and nonverbally—that you value them and that you love them unconditionally.

Soothing: Being Their Calm

Being in the presence of a calm, warm, and caring person makes us feel better—and this is especially true for adolescents, whose brains are still developing the capacity for self-regulation. The teenage brain is undergoing massive reconstruction, and the areas responsible for emotional control are among the last to fully mature. This means your teenager genuinely needs your help staying regulated, even when they insist they do not.

Children and adolescents are not yet skilled at soothing themselves. This ability grows with time, and every time you soothe them, you strengthen their own capacity to self-soothe. Scientists call this co-regulation: your calm nervous system helps regulate their activated one. Your calm presence literally helps their nervous system develop the pathways it needs for self-regulation. When anyone is struggling—

child or adult—connection is often the answer. Before problem-solving, before advice, before correction, offer your calming presence.

Understanding: Seeing Through Their Eyes

When you are having a hard time, having someone who listens and truly tries to understand makes all the difference. When a person gets you—really gets you—it creates closeness. Your teenager is no different, even if they roll their eyes when you try.

Try to put yourself in your teen's shoes—see situations from their perspective. This is empathy in action. For example, imagine you have asked your child to put down their phone and start homework, but a few minutes later they are still chatting with friends. Your frustration rises. But consider: stopping something enjoyable is genuinely hard—for anyone. And starting homework, which is usually not fun and may feel overwhelming, is even harder. Your teen is not trying to defy you; they are struggling with a difficult transition. Understanding does not mean excusing the behavior or abandoning your expectation; it means responding from a place of connection rather than frustration. You can still insist on homework while acknowledging that the transition is hard.

Enjoyable Activities: The Glue of Connection

We simply like people we have a good time with. This is as true for teenagers as it is for adults. When you laugh together, oxytocin is released, binding you closer. Shared joy creates shared memories, and those memories become the fabric of your relationship.

These activities do not need to be elaborate or expensive: watching a series together, going for a walk in the park, kicking a ball around in the garden, playing a quick card game, cooking a meal side by side, or simply sharing a hot chocolate while chatting about nothing in particular. With work and household responsibilities, finding spare time can be difficult—but regular small moments count just as much as big outings. Ten minutes of genuine connection every day adds up to more than an occasional special event.

If your relationship needs strengthening and you are not sure where to start, begin small. Put a plate of biscuits or a favorite drink next to where your child is sitting. Sit near them while they do something, even if you are just reading nearby. Comment with interest on something they care about. All the small building blocks count. Connection is built one moment at a time.

The Bridge That Carries Everything

We could summarize it from a teen's perspective:

I have a good relationship with my parents because I can see they love me. They are there for me when I struggle. They try to understand me. They speak kindly to me. And we have a good time together.

This may seem like a lot to implement, but I assure you—as a parent of a teen myself—it is truly doable. You do not have to be perfect. You just have to be consistent in your efforts and willing to repair when you fall short. And what you receive in return—their trust, their openness, their affection—makes parenting not only easier but genuinely enjoyable.

A strong connection will also make your child want you present in their life long after they move out—when the choice is completely theirs. The relationship you build now is the relationship you will have for the rest of your lives.

For those of you already applying these principles, you are doing important work—work that will echo through generations. And for those just beginning, know that every small step toward connection is a step worth taking. Start today. Start small. But start. Your relationship is the foundation upon which everything else rests.

Amélie Friedrich is a clinical psychologist certified in child and adolescent therapy with over fifteen years of experience as a psychological and educational counselor in schools. She now works with parents navigating challenges related to big emotions, high sensitivity, behavior, sleep, and picky eating in young children. Guided by neuroscience, Amélie provides evidence-based information and practical strategies that help families thrive. Learn more at www.ameliefriedrich.com.

BRIDGING THE RELATIONSHIP: WHEN MANAGING GIVES WAY TO LEADING TWEENS & TEENS

Jayme Harrison

"No."

A tiny two-letter word.

You've heard it before from that toddler, planted firmly on the floor, the preschooler testing limits, the small child discovering their will. Back then, the "no" felt loud, dramatic, almost predictable, and your heart warmed slightly with pride. It came from a child who needed you to decide, direct, and interpret the world for them. You explained. You reasoned. You guided. And it worked......well, most of the time.

But this "NO" is different.

This one lands in your body before it reaches your ears. It's quieter. Firmer. Heavier. It comes from a child who is bigger now, not just in size, but in mind, opinion, and identity. A child who can walk away. Shut down. Push back. A child whose nervous system is growing and learning where its edges are.

This isn't the same "no" you could redirect or override.

This isn't about defiance or attitude.

This is no longer a "no" you can manage your way past.

In the earlier years, parenting created safety and connection largely through managing your child. You organized, guided, and decided almost everything your child did, when and how they did it, and why. That structure quietly formed a bridge, keeping you close and actively escorting them across. Through management, the connection between you and your child grew—what we call attachment—because you were containing the world for them, holding what they could not yet hold on their own.

And it mattered. Deeply.

But as your child moves into the tween and teen years, something shifts. Logic and explanation start to fall flat as emotions surge and overwhelm takes hold. Behavior becomes harder to predict and harder to control. The more you try to manage your way back to what once worked, the more the bridge can begin to feel less safe. Not because you're doing it wrong, but because connection is shifting from being built through leading, not managing.

I know this through my professional work supporting children and families with diverse ways of thinking, feeling, and regulating. And I live it daily as a parent navigating this same shift with my own children.

This chapter isn't about building a bridge from scratch. It's about evolving the bridge you already have to support your growing child.

For most parents, this shift doesn't arrive all at once. It shows up in the everyday rhythms of family life; more "no's" around leaving the house, screens, bedtime, homework. It's the refusal to talk when you ask what's wrong, followed by an emotional outburst later. One moment you're walking on eggshells, the next you're locked in a power struggle. The child you once felt so connected to now feels unpredictable, distant, or constantly overwhelmed—and you're left wondering when things became so hard.

Let me share an experience of this in my house.

The Homework Standoff

I knock on the closed door and crack it open just enough to fit my head through. My daughter is at her desk. Laptop open. Chair tilted. One foot tucked up on the seat.

"Hey. Homework getting done?"

She barely looks up. I hear the eye roll. "No."

And without thinking, I'm in the room. I explain that homework must be done. That school expects it. She'll get into trouble. Question: What's the problem? It's only 10 minutes. Come upstairs, and I'll help. I'm being supportive.

Each sentence is logical. Reasonable. Well-intentioned.

This isn't support. It's management. I'm leaning hard on logic and direction, thinking that more of the same will push us through because I'm not sure what else to do.

What's happening is something very different.

Her nervous system is overloaded. My words feel like pressure, not help. Shame creeps in. Confidence drops. Frustration rises. Homework becomes charged—not just with work, but with our relationship.

And the bridge between us starts to crack.

What was once a safe crossing begins to feel like a checkpoint. The cost isn't just unfinished homework. It's a child who feels less safe, less connected, and less attached in a relationship that carries strain it doesn't need to.

The reality is the bridge is under pressure, and something needs to shift.

This is where you evolve to BRIDGE the relationship with your teen.

BRIDGE

When I talk about the bridge, I'm talking about the relationship you've already built.

When I talk about BRIDGE, I'm talking about how you learn to *hold and lead within that relationship* during the tween and teen years.

As children grow, their developmental capacity for independent thinking expands, their emotional world intensifies, and their external world becomes more complex and demanding. The old parenting bridge built around compliance and control simply won't carry the same weight.

BRIDGE is not about abandoning boundaries or lowering expectations. It is about recognizing that leading is a stronger foundation to be steady, predictable, and strong enough to hold tension, disagreement, and repair for teens.

At its core, BRIDGE is a discipline of leadership. Discipline in the truest sense of the word—teaching. Take it in, parents. You are your child's greatest influence and role model! Your state of mind, your regulation, and your capacity to see and to think differently are powerful. It shapes how you connect with your child. BRIDGE is not a model reserved for major blow-ups or crisis moments. It's equally powerful in the ordinary, repetitive interactions where patterns are formed.

Let me be clear—this isn't a quick fix where everything suddenly improves. While you will see small shifts, BRIDGE is a kind of change that happens over time, in everyday moments where you pause instead of push. It's a practice of easing out of automatic managing and learning to lead with your child, one interaction at a time.

What BRIDGE creates over time is an environment where connection can grow, even as your child pushes away.

BRIDGE is a relationship-led parenting approach for the tween and teen years, when managing no longer creates safety in the same way. What management once held, leadership must now hold.

BRIDGE breaks this shift down into moments—how you steady yourself, read what's really happening, choose the relationship, decide how to lead, go back to reflect, and evolve how the relationship is held over time.

B - Be Steady First

Before anything else, BRIDGE begins with you.

Staying steady is hardest when your teen's behavior sparks frustration—when that "no" presses familiar buttons. Yet steadiness isn't about staying calm or being permissive. It's about not becoming another source of threat in an already overloaded moment.

In the homework standoff, this might look like pausing at the doorway instead of storming in. It might sound like, "Okay. Noted," followed by stepping away. This won't magically create cooperation, yet over time your steadiness becomes familiar—something your child can lean on even when they push back.

R - Read the Moment, Not Just the Behavior

In this stage of development, behavior is rarely about defiance. It's information. Overwhelm, fatigue, fear of getting it wrong, pressure, loss of control can all show up as "No".

Reading the moment means looking beneath the behavior to capacity, not excusing it; instead, understanding what's shaping it. Instead of "What's your problem with homework?" you shift to, "Is this too much right now, or is it the homework itself?"

You may not get an answer, and that's okay. Wait, as this moment is for you to interpret what's happening. If you can't read it yet, park it with "We'll come back to this later."

I – Hold Your Intent on the Relationship

Connection isn't automatic. It's chosen.

Holding relational intent means deciding—often silently—that protecting the relationship matters more than winning the moment. This is the internal shift from managing to leading.

In a homework standoff, it might sound like, "Homework matters. Our relationship matters too. We'll figure this out without a fight."

Tweens and teens don't need parents who agree with them—they need parents who can stay connected while disagreeing.

If you hear yourself lecturing, that's your cue:

"I'm talking too much."

D - Decide How to Lead

Leading in this moment means choosing to hold space and resisting control. It's about staying steady and clear while allowing your child to find their way through.

In a homework moment, you might say, "Homework needs attention, and I trust we can work out how that happens." This respects autonomy while still supporting accountability—not through pressure, but through the relationship.

Leading recognizes differences in capacity, timing, and regulation, and responds to what your child needs in that moment, not what feels easiest for you. Leading is not perfection—it's never too late to pause, reset, and do something differently.

G - Go Back and Reflect

Later matters.

Going back is where reflection, repair, and reinforcement live.

Repair teaches that conflict doesn't end connection. "Earlier, homework got tense. I didn't handle it well, and I don't want homework to be like a fight between us."

Reinforcement recognizes moments that nurture it. "I like hearing about your homework, even though you find it annoying."

Teens rarely give you a movie-style heart-to-heart. You're looking for small signs like less shutdown or defensiveness, and more willingness to try another time.

If they refuse the conversation, respond with "Okay. I'm here when you're ready." Then go back again later.

E - Evolve & Embed the Relationship

BRIDGE asks you to evolve how you lead—not to give in.

There's no denying it. Nothing stays the same.

If homework standoffs continue, evolve your thinking. Once you read the moment, you'll see where things could change, and you can lead differently. This might sound like "This doesn't seem to be working. Let's find another way."

If you slide back into management, begin again at B.

Common Challenges

Even with the best intentions, real life will test the BRIDGE approach—especially when time pressure, fatigue, and emotion are already high. BRIDGE isn't a step-by-step sequence. Its elements overlap and cycle. At different moments, you may be steady first, read later, go back sooner—all of it matters for connection and attachment.

One common challenge is being pulled back into managing when nothing seems to move. It's tempting to assume leading isn't working and to tighten control. Always return to the BRIDGE. Don't burn it!

On hard nights, shorten the task, postpone, or decide that connection matters more right now.

Leading doesn't mean stepping away from responsibility. In moments of safety, risk, or well-being, your child may need you to lead decisively. This doesn't crack the bridge; how you go back afterward is what strengthens it.

Choosing which battles to fight can also be hard. BRIDGE isn't about getting it right every time. It's about staying in the work and noticing the small wins as leading takes shape.

Homework standoffs still happen for me. But it now includes moments when she chooses to do it herself, then comes back to tell me how annoying it was, which often turns into what she learned. That return matters. That's attachment. And as a parent, it feels amazing and still surprising.

Holding What Matters

Parenting tweens and teens asks something different of us. The bridge you built through years of managing still matters—but it now needs to be held through leadership, regulation, and relationship. BRIDGE reminds us that safety comes first, that behavior is information, and that repair strengthens connection more than control ever could.

If there's one thing to try today, let it be this: begin with B. Stay steady.

Leading through this stage isn't about getting it perfect—it's about bridging the relationship with your teen.

If you'd like to go deeper, explore my family resources, workshops, or programs designed to strengthen the bridge through the tween and teen years.

Jayme Harrison is a Family Life Coach, neuro-affirming practitioner, and accredited Circle of Security Parenting facilitator specializing in preventative well-being and early intervention. With over 20 years of experience spanning government to entrepreneurship, she founded Teacup Coach in Brisbane, Australia, delivering evidence-informed well-being programs and coaching for children, teens, and their families. Extending her expertise through a Master's in Counseling and Psychotherapy, Jayme strengthens parent-child connection while building confidence, resilience, and self-esteem in young people. Living in the city and retreating to the family farm with her two teens on weekends, she believes prevention is powerful and that nurturing connection and well-being early helps families thrive. Explore her programs and resources at www.teacupcoach.com.

WHY YOUR TEEN DOESN'T WANT YOUR ADVICE & WHAT TO DO INSTEAD

Cecilia and Jason Hilkey

When Jason and I were first married, he had more kitchen experience than I did. One time when I was using a pasta spoon to stir soup, he would "kindly" say, "That tool isn't intended to be used that way."

Jason's unsolicited advice did not land well with me. My inner two-year-old wanted to stomp her feet and prove him wrong.

When parenting our teens, I sometimes do "a Jason" and become the well-intended advice-giver.

I look at our teens, and I think, "If they'd just do what I told them to do, all their problems would be solved."

I imagine that, after hearing my wise counsel, they will say, "Mom, you are a genius."

I will say, "I know, right?"

"Thank you. I love you so much."

"I love you too, darling."

But this isn't how it works in real life.

When I give our teens advice, I don't get gratitude; I get resistance.

"Mom, that won't work."

So I offer *more* advice, solutions, and anything to help.

"I bought you a [thing to fix it]." or "We'll hire a tutor."

"Mom, you don't understand. That idea is dumb [boring, or stupid]."

If I get scared, I might say something like, "That's it. I'm taking away your phone until your homework is finished," or something I will regret comes out like, "If you don't figure this out, you're going to be flipping burgers your whole life."

Then, our teen explodes, "Leave me alone!" or quietly implodes, "I'm broken, I can never get this right."

What Teens Actually Want

We all want our teens to succeed. We'll do anything we can to help. But the more we try to help, the more they push back (just like I did with Jason's cooking advice).

How can we just "get our teens to listen"?

First, let's look at some recent research on the emotional lives of teenagers, the coping strategies they turn to when they're upset, and what support they are looking for from adults.

In a major survey conducted by Dr. Lisa Damour in partnership with Gallup and the Walton Family Foundation[4], researchers asked teens, "When you get upset, what do you typically want your parents or caregivers to do?"

More than anything, upset teens want adults to listen and take their feelings seriously.

Caring adults, the survey showed, are often inclined to offer advice, but...

Advice is not what upset teens are usually looking for.

From Advice-Giver to Coach

Now, you might be wondering, "But how can I help my teen when they are struggling and upset, if I'm not supposed to offer advice? How do I listen to their feelings when my teen isn't doing the right thing and won't even talk to me?"

The key to becoming the kind of parent that our teen also wants (and needs) is a simple (but not always easy) shift. Teens are more likely to be motivated, take charge of their problems, and start talking to us when we shift from an advice-giving to a coaching role.

The easiest way to shift into a coaching role is by changing one simple thing... You start asking your teen questions.

Asking questions encourages teens to do their own problem-solving and critical thinking. When teens come up with a solution on their own, they are more likely to follow through with it. And if they chose *their* solution—not yours—they can't blame you if it doesn't work out (ask us how we know this).

Asking questions (without giving advice) also sends teens an important, implied message. It says, "You can handle this. You have the skills to figure this out. You're gonna be okay." Even if your teen isn't great at solving their problems yet, they will feel supported by you. Your belief in your teen could be a powerful motivator—especially when they might not believe in themselves.

What This Sounds Like in Practice

Let's talk a little bit about what these two different approaches sound like in practice, with some examples. Pretend your teen is struggling with their homework, and naturally, you're tempted to jump in and give advice. Here's what you can say instead to shift into a coaching role.

"Advice Giving" Parent says	"Coaching" Parent says
"I got you a calendar so you can keep track of all your assignments."	"You've said you have trouble keeping track of your assignments. What do you think would help?"
"You can't be on that screen until you've finished your homework."	"What's your plan for finishing your homework?"
"Here's what you should do…"	"What have you already tried so far?" "What worked when you faced a situation like this in the past?"

"Advice Giving" Parent says	"Coaching" Parent says
"You've gotta put your phone away, otherwise you'll get distracted."	"If I see you get distracted by your phone, what is the least annoying way for me to support you?"
"You just need to sit down and concentrate. Try harder."	"What are your ideas for how to solve this?" or "Which of these options do you hate the least?"
"We'll hire a tutor."	"Do you think a tutor would be helpful? What pros and cons do you see?"

The Questions Every Parent Asks

When parents think of shifting from "advice giving" to "coaching," there are some concerns that often come up.

"What if my teen's solution doesn't work?"

Sometimes teens, despite our best efforts, will choose something that we're pretty sure won't work. I hate to say this... those opportunities, when teens fail in small ways, are fantastic for learning. I know it's very difficult to watch teens make mistakes, but we're not talking about "tough love" or standing by idly while your teen sinks. You can still support them every step of the way while letting them figure it out.

Here are some ideas about how to support your teen while still honoring their autonomy:

- **Check in.** "Let's check in, in a couple of days [or weeks], to discuss which parts of this plan are working and which parts you want to change."

- **Define what "success" looks like.** "How do we know that this plan is working?" "How will we know if this plan is not working and that we need to do something else?"

- **Define where the boundaries are.** "I'm willing for you to do it your way for 2 weeks. After that, if you're still missing assignments, let's have another conversation."

Treat this like a science experiment where your teen is testing out new theories and adapting. As long as your teen's solution doesn't put them in danger or interfere with you doing the things you need to do, consider letting them try to do it their way. The point is for your teen to try new things until they discover what works for them and what really doesn't.

"My teen won't talk to me."

Sometimes, when parents shift from advice-giving to coaching, their child won't want to talk, or they'll answer, "I don't know." When teens don't talk to adults, it often says more about us, parents, than about the teens. Our own kids can always tell if we have an agenda, a solution we're going to push, or if we are angry or scared. Generally, if caring adults are open and receptive, teens do want to share their thoughts and feelings.

The two things that shut down a conversation the quickest are: if teens think they will get in trouble, or if they think that talking to us will make us feel scared or upset. It's understandable for us parents to feel worried, upset, or tempted to punish; those reactions will rarely create the kind of connection and closeness that allows our teen to open up and share what is going on in their life.

If your teen won't talk to you, try telling them this: "We've drifted apart, and I'd like to be closer. Is there something I could do differently to make it easier for you to talk openly with me? Or did I mess something up in the past? If you tell me, I won't get upset or offended, and you won't be in trouble."

Then listen to what your teen says.

"What if my teen doesn't have any solutions?"

Sometimes a parent will ask their teen, "What is your plan to solve this?" and the teen says, "I don't know." If a teen doesn't have any ideas, you ask, "Do you want to hear some of mine?"

Once you've gotten permission, you can share your solutions. Getting permission is key for a teen to have buy-in and follow through.

There are three additional reasons for teens to say, "I don't know."

1. "I don't know" could be code for: "I'm too overwhelmed, or embarrassed; I think I should know how to do this. I feel like I'm failing." If you think your teen is having these feelings, you can say, "Look, you don't need to beat yourself up over this. It makes sense that you'd be figuring this stuff out. There are lots of adults who haven't figured all this stuff out yet."

2. "I don't know" could be code for: "You don't listen/trust/support my ideas." If this is the case, go back and read the section *"My teen won't talk to me."*

3. "I don't know" could be code for: "I've already considered all of the options, and they all suck." If your teen doesn't like any of the available solutions, keep reading...

"What if my teen doesn't like any of the solutions that are available?"

Sometimes, despite your best efforts, you and your teen still might not come up with a solution that feels good to both of you. If you find yourself stuck, here are a few things to offer. Notice that each of these is phrased as a question, so your teen—not you—is in charge.

Take a break. Come back to it later.

- Parent says, "Seems like we haven't figured out any good solutions yet. Can we take a break and come back later?"

Ask someone else for help:

- Parent says, "Is there someone you respect who could help or offer a new perspective? Maybe a teacher, older friend, or relative?"

Think of a third way:

- Parent says, "Is there an outside-the-box solution that we haven't considered yet?" Example: In our own family, after a lot of effort, conversation, and trying out different solutions, one of our teens couldn't figure out how to make high school work for them. In the end, our teen decided to get a GED and go to work instead. Now, as a young adult, on their own terms, they've started college.

Pick the best of the options, even if it's not ideal:

- Parent says, "This could be one of those times when none of the options are great. If you had to pick now, which option do you hate the least?"

What About When It's Not Safe to Step Back?

All of this assumes your teen's choices are within the realm of normal trial and error. But what about the moments that feel genuinely unsafe?

There are times when we set limits without asking questions and without getting feedback from our kids. If a car is barreling down the road headed toward your teen, of course, you do whatever you can to keep them safe. In our family, our non-negotiables include everyone wearing a seatbelt in a moving car and no underage substance use inside our house. Ideally, you can explain your limits and the reason for them beforehand and answer your teen's questions.

Coaching (Not Correction) Increases Connection

Remember, your teen wants you to listen and to take their feelings seriously. If you're tempted to offer advice, try asking your teen a question instead. Asking questions puts you in the coaching role and keeps your teen in the driver's seat of their life. Chances are, if you can listen without jumping in to fix things, your teen will talk more to you, be more motivated, be more invested in solving their own problems, and feel more connected to you. And you may find that the connection you've been working so hard to build was waiting on the other side of the question.

And thankfully, Jason has (mostly) stopped giving me advice about the proper way to use the kitchen utensils.

Cecilia and Jason Hilkey co-founded Happily Family in 2012. The mission of their online conferences and courses—which help over 100k parents each week—is to maintain the connection between our kids and ourselves, even during tough moments. They help parents navigate the beautiful mess of family life by sharing their experience raising three kids, their work in early childhood education, and their therapy for high-needs kids. Parenting is hard, especially during the teen years. Make it easier by getting FREE access to 25 parenting experts on tweens and teens when you scan the QR code.

KNOW YOUR ROLE

Clair Goodman White, MA

I did it again. I left another tense conversation with my teen, carrying a crushing feeling of defeat. Not defeated by my kid, but by my own impulsivity, my inability to keep my cool, and approach a delicate conversation strategically. I jumped in, unprepared and uncouth.

Before we even began the exchange, I bubbled with resentment, irritation, and overwhelming negativity. I focused on how I'd been wronged. I know better than to engage when I'm approaching attack mode. I did it anyway. *That*—my own lack of self-control—annoyed me far more than anything my teen said or did!

My mistake: I responded before I was ready and engaged while emotionally charged. I know not to address anything sensitive until I'm fully ready.

But What Does "Ready" Mean?

Ready means being intentional, choosing how I'm going to show up for my kids. It means strategically selecting the role I play as a parent, especially during delicate moments. Being ready means thinking ahead and beyond my own needs and impulses.

I wanted to prioritize my teen's desires and be a presence she welcomed, but I got in my own way. I let my emotions get the better of me, believed I knew her needs better than she did, and struggled to put aside the ideal parent I always envisioned I'd be.

The Parts Parents Play

As a new mom, I thoughtfully considered what kind of parent I would be, then prepared to play that part for the rest of my life. My infant promptly became a toddler, and I veered from that vision, not always the parent I intended. Preschool brought more changes, not just in my daughter but in me, too. With each age and stage, we both developed. I frequently found myself playing unfamiliar and unplanned roles.

Consistency is essential, but kids constantly change. Especially with teens, parenting means reading the room, the mood, the behavior, and responding to whatever reality calls for. I've played various roles throughout my kids' lives. Without a doubt, adolescence requires the most frequent and unanticipated shifts. Reading the room and meeting teens in each moment is like family improv. When we get it right, it flows. When we don't, it's tense and awkward.

I've learned that when teens:

...vent, they need an open ear, someone to stay quiet and listen, while occasionally validating.

...emote, they want a comforter, perhaps with a hug, a favorite meal, hot cocoa, or movie night.

...externally process, they desire a silent sounding board, someone to let them process out loud without giving input.

...ask for advice, they want another to understand before providing thoughts and ideas, to make suggestions, not demands.

...ask for help, they want specific support, not whatever others are willing to give.

Teens want to connect and open up. The challenge is getting adults to show up in ways that facilitate connection. I want to be someone my kid chooses to engage with; someone they move toward. Not emotionally reactive, uncontrolled, or self-focused (as I gracelessly demonstrated above), I want to show up for her. The parts aren't complicated, and teens are pretty clear about what they want—or, more often, what they don't want. Moment to moment, I simply read the need and thoughtfully choose my role.

With a fair amount of trial and error, I've found some roles consistently make or break conversational flow with teens. I don't always get it right, but these distinctions have helped me through some touchy teen talks.

Listener vs. Lecturer

When it comes to sensitive teen topics—friendships, crushes, intimacy, parties—I want to hear what teens have to say. Always. Yet oftentimes, as soon as my kids open up, I interrupt. I shift the focus to what I have to say, launching into a monologue that teaches valid and important points they don't hear because my timing is off. I become the speaker instead of the listener. They disengage; we disconnect; the conversation ends.

There's a difference between talking *with* kids and talking *to* or *at* them. Slipping into lecture mode is natural and automatic—a habit that gets in the way of us having the reciprocal conversations I crave. Of course, there are times when my teens need guidance or a reality check. Even in those moments, they're far more receptive and open when we have a back-and-forth conversation.

When I shift my focus from imparting wisdom to creating an inviting and comfortable space for them to be heard, they open up. I listen more. They talk more. I let go of the pressure to be all-knowing or have the right answers. Sometimes they aren't looking for answers. They're looking for an available ear or sounding board, someone who won't judge, interrupt, or get involved. When that's the parent they want, that's the parent I want to be.

As a listener, I let them have the spotlight and give them my undivided attention. I encourage them to share their stories, rather than jumping in with advice. I become the audience and allow them the speaking parts. It takes tremendous strength to tamp down my inner monologue. That's my work to do. It's incredible how much they share when I show interest, get quiet, and listen well.

Confidante vs. Judge

I love when kids see me as someone safe to confide in, trustworthy with their thoughts and feelings. So why is my knee-jerk response the one that stops them from opening up? When my daughter talks about typical teen drama (especially "mean girl" stuff!), I jump in with judgment. I criticize her friends, and she ends up defending the very people who hurt her! Instead of feeling supported and validated, she feels attacked. Not surprisingly, the confiding stops.

In mindful moments, I request a do-over. It takes self-control, but I *can* listen well, hold my opinions inside, and allow her uninterrupted, impartial airtime to vent. This gives her space to express herself, which is what both of us most desire. I'm not sitting stone-faced and silent. I reflect back to her what I heard. Without inserting snarky commentary, I share my understanding of what happened. I focus on her feelings and reactions, not my own.

My teen's experience takes center stage and leads our conversation. When she trusts me not to evaluate her and her friends, she shares more openly. We talk about sensitive and private things without her feeling judged. We experience a genuine, deep connection rooted in mutual trust, respect, and acceptance. When she wants a trustworthy and nonjudgmental confidante, that's exactly the parent I want to be.

Supporter vs. Solver

I'm hardwired to fix my kids' problems. I don't want them to suffer, feel disappointment, or get hurt. Since I can't bubble-wrap my teens to prevent harm, I attempt to minimize their upset as soon as they face challenges. I insert myself and fix what's broken. I'm an excellent problem solver, and they don't have fully developed brains, so of course, I need to step in and fix everything, right?

Despite my wealth of knowledge and decades of experience, my teens usually balk at my involvement. Initially flabbergasted that they reject such heartfelt (and, let's face it, *invaluable*) assistance, I realize the rub: they aren't asking for my help. They don't want my involvement. They want someone to lean on. They want to feel secure.

Oh, the times they ask for a little help on a school project, and I inadvertently take over! I believe I'm helping, but their discouragement and disappointment are palpable. As my presence fills the room, their energy and enthusiasm fade. So often, I walk away either resentful that they don't appreciate my assistance or deflated because I've demoralized my perfectly capable kid.

When my teens come to me with challenges, I desperately want to shield them from pain or hardship. My protective instincts kick in. It takes everything in me to resist the urge to shield and shelter. Without those challenges, though, they won't learn. Telling doesn't teach. Experience does. To raise capable, independent, responsible humans, I have to let them fail, fall, and figure things out. My role as a teen's parent is to provide support, not to prevent or problem-solve for them. When I jump in to do that, I rob them of the opportunity that serves them best in life—to learn how to solve their own problems.

Instead, during those vulnerable moments when they approach me with a dilemma, I remind myself to hold back. I guide them gently by asking open-ended questions, exploring their thoughts, clarifying their preferences, and helping them generate their own solutions. We ponder their options, and they evaluate consequences. *They* figure things out. *They* choose what's best for them. They get the joy of impressing others with their hard work and sheer brilliance. I feel immensely proud of them and satisfied for them.

Storyteller vs. Advisor

Teens love hearing about my past...when I choose the right moments to share. They find my tales of adolescent antics, mishaps, and tomfoolery amusing. For them, it's all about entertainment and connection, learning who I am, the teen I was, and the ridiculous things I've done.

Their reactions are less charitable when I share my stories with ulterior motives. When my teens confide in me about familiar struggles, my instinct is to empathize—connecting their situation with my childhood experiences. Those attempts to relate often backfire. They voice a classic "you don't know how it feels" response and quickly shut down the conversation.

My ancient trials don't compare with my teens' current challenges. The more I try to make those connections, the more distant they become. My attempts to communicate understanding leave them feeling invalidated. I walk away discouraged and misunderstood. They leave feeling exactly the same.

In what appear to be "teachable moments," I use cautionary stories like Aesop's fables. Teens resent advice subtly veiled in parent lore. They see through my lessons, dressed in childhood anecdotes, and justifiably push back. Apparently, I am the one needing to learn a lesson!

After many missteps, I finally got it: Teens enjoy learning *about* my experiences, not always *from* them.

I didn't give up teaching through my experiences but learned when they are welcome. The key is sharing in ordinary, uncharged moments. Teens are more open to learning from adult mistakes when the stories aren't loaded, and emotions aren't high. So I tell my stories randomly.

As we laugh together about my childhood shenanigans, they learn, we connect, and they hold onto family memories. That's what I was hoping for all along.

Multiple Roles, Not Multiple Personalities

As my role changes over time, my personality does not. I don't shape-shift or take on a new persona. I'm myself, my teens' parent, showing up in the way they need me most. I move toward them, and they approach me more often. They're comfortable coming to me with different needs and desires because I'm willing to provide what they are looking for, not what I want to provide or what I think they need.

If I could go back in time, I'd encourage me-as-a-baby-parent to hold onto those intentions loosely; to flex, adapt, and adopt new roles as new needs arise. No parent of a newborn can fathom what it takes to connect with their teen. Parenting is about growing alongside our kids. I didn't just shape my kids. They shaped me and my understanding of my role as a parent. Thank goodness they did. We're all better for it!

Clair Goodman White, MA, owns Clair White Coaching, a wellness and parent coaching practice in Indianapolis, Indiana. Affectionately known as "The Feelings Teacher," she's also the Social Emotional Coach at a Kindergarten-8th parochial school. Clair leads workshops on all things parenting and wellness, providing practical tips for people of all ages facing everyday stressors. Trained in clinical child psychology, she learned most about parenting from her three incredible teenagers. In her spare time, Clair enjoys mindful walks with her husband, coffee with friends, stress-busting workouts, and diving into classic books she should've read in high school.

Get quick tips to connect with teens by scanning the QR code below.

LET CURIOSITY LEAD: A SIMPLE SHIFT THAT HELPS TEENS DEVELOP THEIR INNER COMPASS

Kirsti Kenneth

Just getting everyone to the dinner table feels like a victory. Tonight, at least, the stars have aligned: We're all home, the table is clear enough to fit our plates, and everyone's happy with the menu (thank goodness for tacos).

Once blood sugar levels are up, I attempt a delicate maneuver: coaxing out a real conversation.

"So... how was school?"

"Fine." My teen gives his standard reply.

That's okay. I've soaked up the parenting advice on this. I need to ask specific questions.

"What are you learning about in history?"

"The Louisiana Purchase."

A non-generic answer! We're getting somewhere.

I lean in with a gentle follow-up, trying to invite a little critical thinking. "Do you think Thomas Jefferson... " Before I even finish the sentence, I'm met with the dreaded eye roll.

His head tilts back. A long, exaggerated sigh fills the space between us. "Mom. Can you not?"

Behind him, I can see five different decks of conversation cards, each promising to unlock meaningful family dialogue. But right now, I feel stuck. And afraid.

Not because anything is *wrong*, exactly. My child is ... fine.

But the spark I assumed would grow naturally within him — the noticing, the wondering, the delight in fresh ideas — seems to be dimming. He's just going through the motions.

Then it dawns on me. In my effort to draw out his curiosity, I have forgotten something essential.

If my son's depth of curiosity and engagement seems flat, maybe it's because I've been a little flat myself.

Curiosity Is Essential – But We Don't Nurture It

Curiosity is not a "nice-to-have" trait. It's essential to identity-building. Curiosity is how young people discover who they are, what they care about, and how they make sense of the world. It's the engine behind meaning, motivation, and self-direction.

We celebrate curiosity in young children when it's cute and harmless and shows up as endless "why" questions. But somewhere along the way, curiosity becomes inconvenient. Risky. Even dangerous.

By the time kids reach their tween and teen years, precisely when curiosity is most needed, it's often treated with suspicion. Better to focus on measurable outcomes for "future success" – get those grades, plan that college path. Our achievement-oriented culture sidelines curiosity.

What does a lack of curiosity look like? It looks like mindless scrolling rather than critical engagement with the content. School becomes something to complete rather than a place to explore. Hobbies fade away. Even high-achieving teens can be adrift. They're busy, capable, even driven, and yet unsure of who they really are.

Curiosity is not about doing extra work or becoming a human encyclopedia. It's about learning to ask questions. In fact, it's about asking so many questions that you get to the ones you can't answer. Learning to grapple with the uncertainties or ambiguities around us is essential. We don't live in a black-and-white world. Curiosity is how we explore all of the grays.

Researcher Todd Kashdan argues that curiosity is not just essential; it's how you create a happy, fulfilling life. And it's a skill you can build.

So if we want our teens to be able to navigate new ideas, wrestle with multi-layered truths, seek out new experiences, and start shaping their sense of self, we have to nurture their curiosity.

Fortunately, the adolescent brain is primed for this if we know how to coax it out. Neuroscience and developmental psychology both show that these years are marked by heightened sensitivity to novelty, a growing capacity for abstract thinking, and a drive for exploration and independence.

So why does my son squash my dinnertime inquiries? Because while the seeds of curiosity are there, they are just that: seeds. Like any life skill, curiosity takes practice. Most kids need a little help for their curiosity to grow into a healthy, empowering skill that equips them for a complicated world.

There's no set window when this has to happen. Many of us rediscover curiosity later in life, often out of necessity. We're encouraged to "notice with curiosity" in parenting, rather than reacting on autopilot. We ask questions to better understand our coworkers and the problems we're tasked with solving. We lean on curiosity as a tool for critical thinking in a complex, overwhelming world.

But what if we helped our teens strengthen their curiosity *now*? And what if it was easier than you think?

Why Managing Doesn't Work—But Modeling Does

As parents, we're wired to manage behavior — to correct, advise, and steer. And there are contexts where that instinct is essential. Teens still need boundaries that help them expand their world safely.

But when it comes to curiosity, managing backfires. You can't really tell a kid to "be more curious" and expect to see any change. The more we push — telling them to "think harder" or asking, "Is that all?" — the more protective walls they will build.

That's because curiosity isn't a behavior to enforce. It's an orientation to the world. And an orientation is learned through modeling, not management.

Modeling means showing—not telling—what it looks like to wonder aloud, notice details, make connections, or sit with uncertainty. It means demonstrating how a curious person moves through daily life instead of trying to coax those behaviors out of others.

This is good news! You can release the feeling that you're in charge of your child's curiosity or that one-word answers mean that you have failed. You can't force it. Instead, you get to turn that energy toward your own habits.

As Todd Kashdan's research has shown, you'll be developing a skill that can bring more happiness and fulfillment to your own life while also helping your teen.

So now for the bad news: the tradeoff is time. Modeling isn't a quick fix. It requires patience and repetition. But it's also how humans have always learned complex life skills.

And I have a simple, practical framework you can use to make curiosity second nature for yourself and, over time, for your whole family.

The Four Ways to Wonder: Simple Lenses to Awaken Curiosity

After yet another conversational dead end at the dinner table, I knew I needed a new approach. I needed a way to spark engagement that didn't rely on interview questions, pressure to perform, or perfectly crafted prompts. Above all, I didn't want it to feel like more work or something extra to add to my already brimming plate.

That work came into focus as The Four Ways to Wonder—four simple lenses you can use anywhere to model curiosity out loud and deepen your own daily experiences in the process.

Think of each lens as a pair of glasses you can slip on to change how you see the world, and then *share* what you notice.

Lens 1: Look Closely

What it means: The world can be fast and loud. For just a moment, slow down and zoom in. Take your time and look for the details you might miss if you rush by.

What it sounds like:

- "I never noticed the tiny flowers on these weeds before."
- "I wonder if that billboard was made with AI. The hands look weird."

Lens 2: Make Connections

What it means: Don't be afraid to think outside the box. Look for the ways that the things around you relate to other things, the broader world, or your own life experience.

What it sounds like:

- "This reminds me of something I did at camp years ago."
- "I'm noticing that the colors on your sweatshirt perfectly match that poster in your room."

Lens 3: Shift Perspectives

What it means: Step away from the outside world and try on a new point of view. Imagine how the space you are in might look through different eyes.

What it sounds like:

- "I wonder what someone from the 1800s would think about a fast food drive-thru."
- "I wonder what your younger self would think about this park."

Lens 4: Find Yourself

What it means: Use your imagination like a mirror. Let the things you see around you inspire you to explore who you are: what you think, what you feel, and what you believe.

What it sounds like:

- "I love this song so much. The sound is so rich; I feel like it wraps around me."
- "That movie made me think about something: I want our family to have real ways that we can give back to our community, doing things that help other people."

You now have everything you need to foster your teen's curiosity and equip them to pursue a full, happy life. Just tuck these phrases into your brain:

- Look Closely
- Make Connections
- Shift Perspectives
- Find Yourself

Then, next time you find yourself killing time in a waiting room, or looking at a garden, or just sitting in your living room, ask yourself:

- What can I notice if I look closely?
- How can I make a connection between two things or ideas?
- How can I shift my perspective?
- What can I find out about myself?

Once you start using the Ways to Wonder in your daily life, you shouldn't expect an instant change. The seeds of curiosity don't sprout overnight. But if you continue to sprinkle them into your routines—looking more closely at that unusual tree on the way to school, or sharing aloud how that TV show connected to one of your core beliefs—you will feel the shift.

Your kids won't immediately jump in with their own revelations. But over time, as you make yourself vulnerable by trying something new and sharing your thoughts, even ideas that seem silly or incomplete, they will pick up on it. Conversations will get a little deeper. In small ways, they'll begin to mirror back your curiosity.

Yes, There Will Be Eye Rolls

Let's be honest: The first time you share an observation out loud, sparked by one of the Ways to Wonder, your teen will roll their eyes. Eye rolls seem to switch on around age 11, and from that point, they're on a hair trigger.

That eye roll doesn't mean you failed—it's armor. It's what people do when they're uncomfortable with vulnerability.

Your job isn't to protect your teen from that discomfort. It's to show them how to move through it.

When you keep modeling curiosity—especially imperfect, unfinished curiosity—you send a powerful message:

- This is a safe space to wonder.

- This is a safe space not to know.

- This is a safe space not to be cool.

And over time, things will shift. Your teen may not jump in right away. But in time, they'll start to take off that armor.

Our family recently went to an art museum. After we finished going through a modern art gallery, I sat on a bench next to my teen. I told him I'd taken photos of the pieces that really grabbed my attention, and I showed him one. The use of color made it look like it was glowing. Then I asked, casually, "Was there any piece that stood out to you?"

"I don't know."

I just waited. I let the silence hang.

"There was this red sculpture. It kind of looked like numbers, or a Nike swoosh."

I swiped to another photo. "This?" He nodded. "It made me think of you, too!"

He smiled a little. And the eye roll was barely perceptible.

Cultivating a Curious Family

Curiosity isn't just good for teens—it's good for *you.*

It deepens conversations. It softens judgment. It brings more texture and meaning into everyday moments.

So just start small. Pick one lens and apply it to something you're already doing *today.*

Take note of how it feels to activate your own curiosity. And if you can, *voice your experience* to your family.

Because every time you choose curiosity — out loud — you're helping your teen develop an inner compass they can carry with them long after the dinner table conversations fade. And that may be one of the greatest gifts you can give them.

Kirsti Kenneth is the creator of *Museumazing*, a family-centered approach to helping parents spark curiosity, creativity, and connection right inside the moments they already have. With a background in curriculum design and museum education, she focuses on small shifts that help families slow down, notice more, and have better conversations, whether they're visiting a museum or at the dinner table. To start practicing the ideas from this chapter, scan the QR code to receive the Museumazing Everyday Wonder Toolkit. It's a free, playful guide with easy prompts you can dip into anytime—no prep, no pressure, just small moments of shared discovery.

THE HEALING POWER OF A LOVE LETTER

Shilpa Kurpad Rao

———

When my daughter was five years old, I wrote her a letter with the intention of working through my own patterns so they wouldn't become hers. Now that she's a tween, I've returned to the practice.

Dear Kiddo,

You are the absolute light of my life. At five years old, even with all of our beautiful and funny conversations, so much of what we share is non-verbal and energetic. I know this world can be so hilarious and exciting, as well as confusing and scary. Sometimes the grownups in your life, like me, make it even more confusing and scary.

Before you were born, most of my life was spent seeking approval from the outside world. I was taught to worry about what other people thought of me and to meet my family's expectations. I trusted other people more than I trusted the little voice inside of me that really knew me.

And then, you were born. I knew I had to start listening to that little voice inside of me because it wasn't just me anymore, it was the two of us! But it felt scary to be different than what everyone expected. You may find this out one day, too... It's really hard to be different in a world that wants you to be the same.

We have had such fun, connected days, and we have had moments of frustration and anger. I wonder if sometimes you thought I was mad at you. I'm sure you did. I am so sorry....it was never, ever you. You were always just being an awesome kid.

I want you to know that while it feels revolutionary to me, I hope the conscious choices I have made in my life feel quite boring to you. I am bridging two cultures and two generations, and I hope the bridge between us will be shorter and filled with laughter and connection. You are the incredible, original you, and I like you just the way you are. I love, love, LOVE being your mama!

Writing this letter was a profound turning point for me in my evolution as a parent. There was something so impactful about writing a letter to my daughter from my heart. It brought so much clarity about the true source of my parental frustration and about my intentions regarding our relationship. It also gave my body the chance to slow down, reflect, and see her more clearly. That our conflicts had much more to do with my inner landscape than with her.

Now, many years later, it is evident that my child is in a new developmental stage. Hello, Adolescence! I have found myself, on more than one occasion, turning into a teenager when I am the recipient of one too many eye rolls or slammed doors.

Apparently, there is still a feisty teenager that lives inside of me, ready to fight when the conditions are right.

So, like I did when my child was very young, I started writing letters again. In doing so, I was able to revisit the internal narratives of my teenage years while incorporating healing, empathy, and deep compassion for my young self and, in turn, for my tween daughter.

The Importance of Letter Writing

As parents, our interactions with our children invite deeper conversations within ourselves. When we witness their struggles, it activates the parts of us that struggled, too.

Writing a letter to our younger selves is a way to reparent ourselves, remembering that we mattered when we were young. When we hold our experiences inside, shame can seep in. Writing allows the embarrassing, humiliating, and traumatic things that happened to rise to the surface, so our wise selves can care for our younger selves with love.

By giving our younger self a voice on the page, we create space to heal the person we used to be. From that softer, more healed place, we can show up for our children as they move through their own teen experiences.

Heartspace letters are especially helpful if you were raised in a family dynamic without healthy boundaries, where love and control were intertwined. A letter to your child naturally separates you from them, allowing you to see both of you as individual yet connected beings.

Sample Letters

First, consider writing to your parents, caregivers, or teachers as your teenage self. Tell them who you were, what you were going through, and what you needed from them. What were your family dynamics like, and how did that affect you? Think about what friendships were like when you were your child's age. What was challenging or confusing for you?

Dear Mom and Dad,

I know I am a lot! Emotions are literally pulsing through me, and I feel like I am overreacting to everything.

You are both so wonderful. You try to be there for me, but I am so erratic, emotional, and all over the place. I want to be alone, but also want comfort. I want to talk, but don't want to listen. I want hugs, but don't want hugs. I love my friends, but sometimes it feels complicated. I hate school, but I know I have to do it. I am scared I won't live up to your expectations.

I push you away, but I just want to be close. I want you to understand me, but I am struggling to communicate in a way that lets us have a conversation.

School is not just academics. It's friends, a social hierarchy, and complying with teachers who are sometimes mean. I don't know what to wear; my body is changing, and I don't know whether to embrace it or think it's not good enough.

I don't feel like I belong anywhere. I don't belong at school. I am one in 800 kids, and I don't even know if the teachers know me. They mistake me for the two other Indian girls at school all the time. And the kids laugh. They ask me if my dad works at a 7-11 or if he's Apu from The Simpsons. My name is different. What we eat at home is different.

I don't feel like I belong at home. Your upbringing, culture, and country were so different. I am trying to live in two worlds.

I keep contorting myself to fit in. Nothing is good enough. You don't under-stand my world. Nothing is fair. Nothing makes sense.

I feel alone.

Next, write to your teenage self as the adult you are now. What did you need to hear from a grown-up when you were 10, 15, or 18 years old? What would a compassionate, empathetic, wise adult have said to you at that time? Someone who saw you for your heart, your good intentions? Saw your pain and how challenging things were for you? What would the softest, most caring love sound like to you?

Dear teenage me,

You beautiful, vibrant, bright light. It was absolutely incredible how you walked through those tumultuous, chaotic years. Middle school and high school were rough. No one acknowledges how brave it is to continue to walk into rooms where you are the only brown person. The only one with a name that the substitute teachers can't pronounce.

You tried so many ways to fit in. Friendships, boyfriends, school clubs, and activities. You felt like you lost yourself sometimes, but now I see – you were never lost, but seeking. Seeking to be seen and accepted. Seeking to rekindle the authenticity you were born with. The you that was buried deep beneath the expectations, multiple identities, the mask of the performative, likeable, smart girl. But, truly deep down, you knew who you were.

The embarrassment, the criticism, the judgment from others, and from your own conditioned mind – I know those feelings and memories stayed within you for a long time. They sometimes informed your choices to stay small or blend into the background.

Your identity was split between two cultures. You wanted to do everything right, but the goalposts were never clear, kept moving, or there were too many to count.

You learned what you didn't want in a life partner. You learned what you couldn't accept in friendship. You learned how you wanted to do it differently if you became a parent one day.

You worked so hard, and you achieved astronomically amazing things. You found your people, you found balance between productivity and fun, and you expanded your mind and the horizons of what is possible.

All while feeling you were not good enough.

You didn't deserve to feel so alone, and yet, your challenges created an incredible diamond. You were remarkable, and I am so grateful for your bravery and resilience.

I love you very, very much.

Finally, carry the same softness and care to your actual child—the tween or teen in your life who is going through the tricky time of adolescence. Consider writing to your teenager from your heart, not to vent, but to empathize and relate. Tell them how much you love them and how much you understand.

Dear Kiddo,

Everything about you absolutely blows me away. You astound me with your brilliance, your kindness, and your creativity. You are this ball of pure love, and I am so profoundly lucky to be your mom.

I see the melancholy sweep over your thoughts sometimes. I see your confidence grow and dip. I see your reactions and feelings grow even when you don't mean for them to.

I want you to know that, while those big feelings sometimes take me by surprise, they are really normal, and I will do my very best not to take them personally. When I make a mistake, I will always repair it with you. You are never alone.

You are forever in my heart, and I am forever in yours. We are always connected. This connection allows you to fly free with a soft place to land.

My teenage experiences were really hard. I am working on making sure that when you have your teenage moments, my inner teenager doesn't show up. You need your calm, patient Mom.

I hope my stories of when I was young, or the work I have put into breaking patterns, are helpful to you. But I hope my story is just that—mine. And you create your own beautiful, vibrant, diverse story.

I respect, admire, trust, love, and adore you. I will always be your number one fan. You are my favorite person in the entire world. Shine that bright light for all to see.

I primarily write letters for my own process and rarely share them with others. Yet the practice of letter writing has helped me repair with my daughter in real time. When we want to apologize, we write to each other. It allows us to slow everything down and get into our heart space before engaging in challenging conversations.

The goal, both with ourselves and with our teens, is not perfection but a safe, compassionate, loving place we can return to again and again. Finding different ways to connect and reconnect is the key, and writing is one of them. Disagreement and conflict are normal; repair protects the relationship in the long term.

Letter writing has been a bridge for me—between my child and me, my past and my present, my mind and my heart. It helps me remember who I was, who I am now, and who I am becoming, alongside my child.

Shilpa Kurpad Rao is a Conscious Parenting Coach dedicated to helping families bridge cultural and generational gaps. She walks alongside clients as they untangle generational patterns and release inherited beliefs that no longer serve them. Over a decade ago, motherhood reshaped Shilpa's path from a doctorate-level scientist to a heart-centered educator for children and parents. She creates healing spaces through one-on-one coaching, group workshops ("The Culture Club"), and online courses. Shilpa lives in Philadelphia, PA, with her awe-inspiring daughter, beloved husband, and adorable dog, Lily.

Visit www.shilparaocoaching.com for a free guide: The Healing Power of a Love Letter: Writing Prompts and Mini-Scripts.

SECTION TWO

THE INNER WORK OF PARENTING

SHIFTING FROM CONTROL TO CREATION: THE INNER WORK OF PARENTING ADOLESCENTS

Casey O'Roarty

———

Are you at the crossroads?

Maybe you were just in your kitchen with your teen, making a reasonable request for help, only to be met with a massive eye roll for the third time today. Or perhaps your kiddo is totally shut down and unwilling to let you in, retreating to their room as much as they can. Or maybe your relationship with your teen has dissolved into angry outbursts, blame, pushback, and the accusation that you are ruining their life.

The season of adolescence is real.

And in these moments, the instinct to fix things, to take control... it comes on *strong*. Which makes sense — we just want the drama and suffering to *stop*. You're the parent. You should be able to *do* something about the way things are going with your young person, right?

But what if this instinct—the one moving you towards trying to control or fix—is actually taking you further from what you really want? Making what already feels really hard... *worse?*

Stay with me here. I want to propose something that may be tough to wrap your head around, especially if you are in the messiness of the teen years.

What if our work isn't about control at all, but about leaning into what we want to create?

Compliance sounds good, I know. Especially on days when nothing you say or do feels helpful. But I am here to invite you to consider a different goal for parenting during the teen years: nurturing critical thinking through a connected relationship.

Here's what I know after raising two of my own kids into young adulthood and working with hundreds of families over the last 20 years — you can't lecture or control your kids into connection or critical thinking. They need space, autonomy, and room to make mistakes and learn from them. They need you to be a soft landing, a curious mentor. They need you to create an environment full of faith in their ability to figure things out. They need you to start with yourself, to regulate and find your own calm. To detach and untangle from their narrative so that they can pave their way, the way they're meant to.

What Do I Know?

I've been where you are. Different details, but the same worry, the same anxiety and fear about what was going on with my teenager.

It was October of 2019. My then 16-year-old daughter had been struggling with mental health for two years. We had just moved to a new town. She decided after 9th grade in public school and 10th grade online that she would enroll in Running Start—a program for high school students in the community college environment.

We were hopeful.

I was at a conference in Atlanta when I got the text: "I'm done with school. I'm dropping out."

This wasn't the first time she had said this, but there was something about the energy of this text. It felt different, final. It activated my whole body, and I knew I had to leave. I needed to be home, with my girl—to, obviously, change her mind.

I couldn't calm my body. The whole trip back to the Pacific Northwest, my stomach was clenched, my thoughts racing. I felt totally out of control. How was I going to get her to change her mind, to recognize life didn't have to be this hard, to SEE that she was making a big mistake?

There were other layers too—substance misuse, disordered eating, extreme anxiety, and depression. I felt very out of my depth…

Me. A parent coach. With the sky falling all around me.

Because she couldn't possibly *drop out of school*. That wasn't part of the plan. I just needed the right words, the right consequences, to push her along, to get her through this without doing too much damage. What kind of future could a high school dropout possibly have? I mean, really?

We Can't Connect or Create Possibilities When We Are Dysregulated

I got home and quickly realized that all the things I had rehearsed during my long plane ride home were worthless. I came home to a child who had made her decision. This was the reality we were in, and my work was to *be with it.*

It's a funny thing—fear, anxiety, dysregulation—it literally prevents you from accessing parts of your brain responsible for connection, curiosity, and creative problem-solving. Your prefrontal cortex goes offline, and your amygdala takes over, pulling you into survival mode—freeze, fight, flight, or fawn.

I engaged in all of them. It was a mess. My nervous system was a mess. And I knew, I knew that nervous system regulation was the foundation of my relationship with my daughter. But I was totally spun out.

Before I go further, I want to be clear about something—being regulated isn't about being calm all the time or never getting emotionally activated by what life throws at you. It's about growing your awareness of the present moment and doing the work to come back to yourself. Recognizing that you are activated and *deciding to create something new.*

This practice of focusing on our nervous system regulation is often skipped in parenting because whatever is happening with our teens feels like a crisis and needs our attention *now*. But I am here to say that who we *be* as we tend to the crisis matters even more.

What Do You Want to Create?

When we are regulated and in the practice of tending to ourselves, we stay connected to the present moment, to what is real and important. This is when we can be intentional about what we want to create in our relationship with our teens. This can feel tricky because it is hard to separate the connection from the behavior you're seeing in your teen. It can feel like approval, or at least like you're not bothered by it. I get that.

It's tender. In my workshops, when I ask parents what's hard right now, I hear things like: *not taking things personally, tolerating their unhappiness and pushback, watching them struggle, letting go of control, and the need to keep them safe.*

Fear is real. Maybe you're afraid they're going to make choices that derail their future. Maybe you're afraid of losing your relationship with them. Maybe their struggles mean, again, that you are failing as a parent. Maybe —and this is a big one—you're afraid that their adolescent behavior is colliding with your dreams for them.

For me, when I was able to get centered and curious about my experience with my daughter, I began to recognize that I was holding a narrative for her that I hadn't seen. I had a vision of her life falling apart, and the unknown was too much. I couldn't see the future. So I got really focused on what I wanted to create in the right now, who I wanted to be for her, and how I could hold space for her to grow through what she was going through.

I wanted more than anything for her to know she was capable. That she would be okay. I wanted her to feel my faith in her. I wanted to create connection, acceptance, and encouragement in our relationship. I wanted her to feel seen and heard. I knew this would serve her more than forcing her—as if I could—onto someone else's timeline.

Over time, this is what helped her help herself. I got better at noticing when I was activated, when my nervous system was spinning me into regrets or catastrophizing about the future, and I worked to come back to the present moment. This is where I could then ask myself, *what do you want to create, Casey? What way of being would be useful right now? What does connection, acceptance, and encouragement feel like, sound like, right now?*

Real Practices That Help

First, start paying regular attention to your nervous system. Adopt daily practices that tune you into the physical sensations alive in you, and work to shift into a state of groundedness. Taking longer exhales than inhales is one way to do this. It lets your nervous system know you are okay. Feel your feet on the floor. Pull your shoulders back. You're okay. You're enough.

Or maybe it's movement. Yoga, a long walk, a bike ride, time in nature. Drink a warm cup of tea or ice-cold water. One parent talked about opening her heart center and her palms when she notices herself shutting down. She physically opens her body as she thinks, *This is the moment to connect.* Can you feel that shift? From closed to open? From controlling to softening?

When we soften into connection, we create a space that, over time, feels safe for our teens to engage in. A space that feels non-judgmental and curious, where they feel heard. Like they matter. This is how we nurture relationship.

If we want them to trust us, we've got to prioritize the relationship.

Being Intentional

Intentionality means taking the time to reflect on the qualities we want to grow in ourselves so that we can be who our kids need us to be. Maybe it's compassion or patience. Maybe it's ease or encouragement. When I work with parents, I encourage them to choose three qualities that will help them be who their kiddos need them to be. These become their "anchor words."

When we're intentional about who we want to be and have words that anchor us, we can catch ourselves in those dysregulated moments and come back to who we want to be. When we lead with compassion, encouragement, and calm, we are creating those qualities in our relationships. Our teens feel it. The relationship shifts. Instead of adversaries, our kids begin to see us as allies.

This is how I moved through the toughest years of parenting my daughter. She did drop out in 11th grade, and there was a period that felt very dark — but we stayed connected. She felt loved and supported through her hardest days. She eventually softened and began seeking support, earned her GED, became a licensed esthetician, and landed a great job. She decided that she wanted more education and started at a community college. She is now a junior at a four-year university, studying biochemistry with her sights on graduate school. She lives on her own and is an incredible human being with a strong sense of self.

We just don't know how things are going to turn out with our teens. But remember that there are endless possible outcomes. And when you take care of yourself, stay focused on who you want to be and what you want to create in your relationship with them, you increase the likelihood that it will all be okay. Maybe even better than okay!

You've got this. I believe in you.

Casey O'Roarty, M.Ed., is a Positive Discipline Trainer, Adolescent Lead at Sproutable, Inc., and the host of the Joyful Courage for Parents of Teens podcast. She is a sought-after speaker and works with parents of teens online through one-on-one coaching and her membership program, Living Joyful Courage. Her book, *Joyful Courage: Calming the Drama and Taking Control of YOUR Parenting Journey*, was published May 20th, 2019. You can learn more about her and her work at www.besproutable.com/teens. Find her on social media @joyful_courage. Casey is thriving in the empty nest with her husband in Bellingham, Washington, and loves any chance she gets to spend time with her amazing young adult kids. Use the QR Code to check out the special offer she created just for you!

PARENTING FROM A REGULATED NERVOUS SYSTEM: WHY YOUR CALM IS THE MOST POWERFUL PARENTING TOOL YOU HAVE

Layne Burkette, LPC, E-RYT

Parenting tweens and teens often happens during the "in-between moments."

In the car—in between activities.

In passing in the kitchen.

In the pauses where they're not quite inviting conversation—but not shutting it down either.

Some of the most meaningful conversations with my teens happen in the car.

No eye contact. No build-up. Just a few honest words offered quietly, almost in passing, as the outside world moves by the windows.

I remember one of those in-between moments. We were driving home from school when one of my teens shared something that caught me off guard. My body reacted first—the tightening in my chest, my hands clutching the steering wheel, the catch in my breath. Almost immediately, my mind followed, rushing to react, question, fix, and protect. Then, my heart hurt. Everything in me wanted to react.

Instead, I paused.

I took a slow breath, felt my feet on the floor of the car, and quietly reminded myself, "I slow down to connect with love." I softened just enough to stay present—with myself and with them.

I didn't rush in with questions or advice.

I listened.

And something important happened.

My teen kept talking.

Moments like that feel like gold—not because we say the perfect thing, but because we stay connected. We don't let our fear or urgency take over the space between us. When we pause and truly listen, our teens feel it.

As a mother of four, and a Licensed Professional Counselor and Somatic Educator, I've seen this truth again and again: The most powerful parenting tool I have isn't knowing the right words.

It's my nervous system.

When we are calm and grounded inside, what I call regulation, we create a sense of safety that our teens can feel. Not safety that comes from control or certainty, but safety that says, "I can stay here with you, even when this is hard."

This chapter is an invitation to return to that steadiness—especially in moments that feel charged—through a simple, embodied sequence I teach and use called Breathe, Move, Heal. These brief micro-pauses help you tend to your nervous system in real time and respond from a place that feels aligned, grounded, and truly you.

When Our Past Shows Up in the Present

Parenting tweens and teens has a way of touching places inside us we didn't realize were still tender. The tone of their voice, a choice they make, a boundary they push—and suddenly our body reacts before our mind has a chance to catch up. Our chest tightens. Thoughts race. We feel the urge to control, correct, or protect.

Often, our strongest reactions aren't about what's happening now, but about what it stirs from our past. Many parents are surprised to discover how much their own teenage experiences still live in their bodies: memories of not being listened to, of feeling misunderstood or unsafe, of being shamed or dismissed. Old fears of being "too much" or "not enough." These experiences don't disappear with time; they become part of our nervous system's memory.

When teens push for independence, struggle emotionally, or make choices that worry us, our old narratives may surface. Without awareness, parents often over-explain, clamp down on control, or shut down emotionally—signs the nervous system has moved outside its window of tolerance. The body responds with more energy (reactivity, urgency) or less energy (withdrawal, shutdown) in an effort to protect.

When we learn to notice these shifts in our bodies and meet them with compassion, then steadiness and presence become possible, growing the capacity to hold experiences with care. The relationship soft-ens, and both parent and teen can breathe a little easier.

One parent I worked with, a caring mother of a 14-year-old, came to me feeling overwhelmed. Her teen had begun pulling away, respond-ing with one-word answers, and shutting down when conversations turned emotional. Homework ended in tension, and check-ins esca-lated quickly.

As we slowed things down, she recognized that her tight body, sharp tone, and guilt about responses were tied to old memories from her own adolescence—feeling unseen and alone. Her nervous system was responding to the past, not the present.

Instead of trying to change her teen, she turned inward. She prac-ticed noticing activation, pausing, and offering herself simple support: a breath, grounding, a reminder that she was safe now. She practiced this in both calm and stressful moments.

Within weeks, conversations softened, her daughter lingered lon-ger, and reactivity decreased. The change came from the parent regu-lating herself, and it rippled outward.

This is the heart of my work: helping people regulate their nervous systems so they can show up with authenticity, compassion, and con-nection—in parenting and in life.

When parents are regulated inside, they have greater access to curiosity, patience, and clarity. They can listen without rushing to fix, allow discomfort, and respond rather than react. Teens feel this shift, often before a word is spoken.

This approach isn't about suppressing emotion or staying calm. It's about offering your nervous system small, intentional support throughout the day. These micro-pauses, practiced consistently, build capacity for presence and regulation.

These micro-pauses follow my simple, embodied rhythm I call Breathe, Move, Heal—a practice for those in-between moments when something tender gets activated.

Real-Life Practice: Parenting from a Regulated Nervous System

At its core, this approach follows a simple rhythm:

Notice ⟶ Pause ⟶ Regulate ⟶ Respond

This isn't a script. It's a loop your body learns over time. Sometimes you'll touch every step. Sometimes one is enough.

Step 1: Slow Down and Notice Activation

The first step is awareness, noticing what's happening inside us. Activation is the moment your body shifts into a state of protection. When your teen says or does something to trigger a response, and you notice:

- A tight chest, clenched jaw, or closed fists

- Holding your breath or breathing shallow

- A sense of urgency or pressure

- A sharper tone creeping into your voice

- The impulse to lecture, fix, question, or shut down

Noticing, *Something is happening in my body,* creates space for choice. Even noticing after the fact counts. Awareness comes first.

Step 2: Pause

Once you notice activation—pause. Even a few seconds matter. This brief pause interrupts the automatic loop between trigger and reaction, giving your nervous system space to settle.

It might look like:

- Silently saying, *"I can* pause."
- Letting one full exhale leave your body
- Softening your shoulders and face

Step 3: Support Your Nervous System (Breathe, Move, Heal)

- Breathe to soften the stress response.
- Move to shift energy in the body.
- Heal with a phrase that brings you back to yourself.

You can take one breath or three, breathe while you move. The phrase can be silent or spoken aloud. If your teen hears you, you're modeling something valuable. The goal isn't perfection; it's offering brief support before responding.

Examples in real moments:

When Your Teen Pushes Back or Resists

(Homework, chores, limits, talking back)

- Breathe: Inhale slowly through the nose, exhale longer through the mouth.
- Move: Press your feet into the floor or gently push your palms together.
- Heal: *I can stay connected without controlling.*

This helps release urgency and soften power struggles before they escalate.

When Your Teen Shares Something Big

(Car conversations, late-night disclosures)

- Breathe: One soft inhale, one long exhale with a soft sigh.
- Move: Hand to heart or gently tap collarbone.
- Heal: *We are safe. I can listen without fixing.*

This signals openness and safety, inviting them to keep talking.

When Old Wounds Get Activated

(Fear, disbelief, anger)

- Breathe: Inhale for 2, exhale for 4.
- Move: Lift and drop the shoulders, gently shake out the arms.

- Heal: *This is old. I am here now.*

This helps separate the past from the present and reduce emotional intensity.

When You are About to React

(Raised voice, shutting down, over-explaining)

- Breathe: Slow belly breath with a long exhale.

- Move: Rise up on toes, drop down onto heels three times.

- Heal: *My calm is their calm.*

This helps to stay present and in your body even when emotions run high.

These moments take 30 to 90 seconds. Over time, your nervous system learns it doesn't have to rush or protect. From regulation, connection, and responding thoughtfully become easier.

Step 4: Respond from Presence

Once your nervous system has settled, even slightly, responses often can be simple:

- "Tell me more."

- "That sounds hard."

- "I'm really glad you told me."

- "This matters. I need a moment, and then I want to talk more."

A neutral, grounded presence keeps the relationship intact—even during hard conversations. Solutions and teaching can wait. Connection comes first.

Practice in Small Moments, Often (and When It Feels Hard)

These micro-pauses work because they are brief and repeatable. Thirty to ninety seconds, practiced consistently, helps your nervous system build a new baseline of steadiness. You don't need long routines or perfect conditions—just small moments, practiced often.

It helps to practice when you're already regulated, outside of stressful moments, so these supports are easier to access when emotions run high. Over time, many parents notice subtle but meaningful shifts: less regret after conversations, quicker recovery after hard moments, and more openness and trust from their teen.

This won't always feel easy. You may forget to pause, notice activation late, or conversations may move faster than your nervous system can keep up with. That doesn't undo the work. Returning to yourself with kindness is a practice, too.

Timing and intensity can both be challenging. Parenting tweens and teens often happens in motion—in the rush out the door, in the car between activities—and emotions can rise quickly. Regulation can happen right there: a breath at a stoplight, feet pressing into the floor while listening, a quiet phrase offered to yourself as your teen talks. When things feel intense, simplify. One long exhale. One grounding movement. One familiar phrase. Regulation doesn't require doing everything—just offering your nervous system something supportive.

I worked with one parent who felt discouraged because she kept "missing" the pause. Instead of giving up, she practiced Breathe, Move, Heal during calm moments, driving alone, waiting in line, and folding laundry. Over time, her body learned the rhythm. When conflict arose, she didn't catch it perfectly, but she caught it sooner. Her teen noticed. Repair came more easily.

Over time, this rhythm—notice, pause, regulate, respond—becomes second nature. Beginning with your own nervous system creates the conditions for calmer conversations, deeper trust, and a more resilient relationship.

Steadiness is built this way—through care, practiced again and again.

Your Nervous System Is Your Greatest Parenting Tool

Parenting tweens and teens doesn't ask us to have all the answers.

It asks us to stay: present when things feel uncertain, connected when emotions rise, grounded enough that our teens feel safe bringing their whole world to us.

Your nervous system is the most powerful parenting tool you have.

Not because it keeps everything calm—but because it helps you remain available. Curious. Steady. Real.

So let today be simple.

When that in-between moment happens—when you feel yourself tighten, rush, or brace—take a breath. Feel your body. Offer yourself one small gesture of support. You don't have to do it perfectly. You only have to stay.

Over time, these moments add up. Conversations soften. Repair comes more easily. Trust deepens, not because you controlled the outcome, but because you stayed connected to yourself.

As the day ends, perhaps once again in the quiet of the car, or as you finally come to rest, pause for a moment. Notice your breath. Notice your body. And listen.

So much of authentic parenting lives here. Not in saying the right thing, but in being

regulated enough to truly listen. Your teens feel this. They feel your presence, your steadiness, your care.

Bring one hand to your heart.

Inhale slowly, exhale softly.

And offer these words—first to your teen:

"I'm here with you, even when this feels hard."

Then, to yourself:

"I'm here with you, even when this feels hard."

Layne Burkette is a life-loving mother of four, a Licensed Professional Counselor, a yoga and somatic teacher, a speaker, and a trainer. She brings warmth, compassion, and embodied wisdom to her work supporting parents, caregivers, professionals, and teams who want to live and parent from a more authentic, aligned place. Layne is also the creator of Breathe, Move, Heal, a nervous-system-based approach integrating breath, movement, and healing affirmations. Begin with her free 5 Days to Calm practice and experience what it feels like to slow down and show up steady and present in the moments that matter most.

IT TAKES A VILLAGE TO RAISE A PARENT

Janey Komm

——

Understanding the biological system from a scientific perspective can serve multiple purposes. Knowledge offers clarity around daily functioning and how to best maintain the body and brain. This creates internal distance, focusing on helping the system through a difficult moment rather than assuming that bad moods or negative reactions are a moral flaw or a personality deficit. Also, the information provides the know-how to respond to psychological injuries with confidence, removing the guesswork. This is important for both caregivers and teenagers. With parenting comes a parallel process. Everything we expect our teens to do, we must be willing and expected to do ourselves.

The Teenage Brain is Under Construction

It's an explosion, and it only happens twice in a lifetime. During the first 24 months of life and again at puberty, the human brain undergoes a burst of neural connectivity. While it is true that the human brain is the most powerful in the animal kingdom, it takes a whopping 25 to 27 years to fully develop. During that time, children experience varying stages of vulnerability and require considerable co-regulation of intense emotions. They are completely dependent on their caregivers to have their needs met. Survival depends on the community's collective support.

Around ages 11 and 12, the brain begins another major reorganization. Adolescence is a transition from dependence to independence, in which the onus of emotional regulation and decision-making shifts from caregivers to the individual. It can be challenging to deal with teenagers who are experimenting with their voices and flexing their muscles. These behaviors are natural tendencies and are positive signs of growth. It is a crucial stage in the development of their identity and is necessary to prepare for the next stage of interdependence in adulthood.

The brain's emotional center—the limbic system—develops before the logical, reasoning frontal lobe of the cerebral cortex. Do you remember when you were 13? One moment you were laughing, the next crying, and then cracking a joke. Emotional cycling can happen rapidly, and the ensuing imbalance surfaces through behaviors such as angry outbursts, bad moods, or pervasive sarcasm. It is like having a turbo-charged race car with no brakes, thrilling and terrifying at the same time. The brakes, namely the frontal lobe, start developing around 16 and don't fully settle until the mid-to-late twenties. This area of the brain is focused on logical reasoning, problem solving, judgment, and rational thought. You can hear the difference when you have a conversation with your thirteen-year-old versus with your seventeen-year-old. There is more access to logic and reason. They are learning self-regulation, self-awareness, and self-determination.

When the Alarm System Takes Over

When the human system feels threatened, the survival brain is activated. This part of the brain is faster and more sophisticated than the logical brain. When stressed, their system floods with cortisol and adrenaline. The body prioritizes immediate survival over long-term functioning, such as digestion and immunity. When stress becomes chronic, and the survival response remains activated, cortisol levels remain elevated. Maybe your teenager is frequently sick or complains of recurring stomach aches and headaches. The body and brain are struggling to stay online. Resetting the survival brain is necessary to send signals of safety to the brain, helping it reabsorb cortisol and flush out excess. Designated rest times and seeking comfort from support systems can help close the loop and allow the system to feel at ease again. The process is personal. Each person becomes their own expert in recognizing when their system is out of balance. Once they recognize things are off, they can re-evaluate and reset. My personal mantra when things don't feel quite right is "I need a nap, a snack, or a pat on the back." While they discover what resets their system, as their caregiver, we can be a part of their recovery if they need to bounce ideas around or a hug. As social creatures, humans always need some form of co-regulation of emotions throughout life. We need each other.

Emotional Capital—A Daily Budget

A significant aspect of maintaining internal homeostasis is understanding and appreciating systemic limitations. Physical limitations are obvious, but emotional limitations are less visible, yet they're just as real.

Imagine someone asked your teen to swim the English Channel next week. Despite their boundless energy, they would hesitate and most likely decline. It would be clear they could not commit to such an athletic adventure without some serious training, effort, or desire. The same level of awareness is not offered to emotional restraints.

I call it emotional capital. We only have $100 a day, not $500 or even $2000. Everything we do requires some amount of emotional expenditure. For example, taking an exam could potentially require $40 of emotional capital, but if it is for a class that is difficult for your teen, that emotional expenditure could jump to $60, and that is not including the rest of the things they are expected to do during the day: Socializing with friends $15; social media $20; work $20; homework $20; sports $15; conflict $15. Some days can really tax their emotional budget when they're maxed out even before they get out of bed. Other days feel more manageable. Helping them identify what is expensive can help them self-determine what a balanced emotional budget looks like.

Just like your teen, your system is spending emotional capital every day, all day long. What feels pricey versus sustainable over days and weeks? Consider a daily parenting budget that may include: household scheduling ($30); work-related emotional expenses ($30); managing family conflict ($20); grocery shopping ($15); paying bills ($20); drop-offs/pick-ups ($20); personal health ($15). You get to decide the amounts. There can be subtle tipping points, such as one too many "I don't like this dinner," or a monumental breaking point, such as debilitating physical sickness when the scales become imbalanced. If we don't take our wellness seriously, an illness will force us to.

Just as there are debits to the emotional bank account, so are there credits. What adds to emotional functioning? Self-care is a daily requirement that can include working out, journaling, setting aside downtime, and unplugging from the digital world, among many other practices. Connection is a healthy deposit, and real-time, face-to-face connections are the most nurturing. Balancing the emotional budget is personal and ongoing throughout life. If you don't know where to start in helping your teen, start with yourself. Modeling for them what internal homeostasis looks, sounds, and feels like can be the most profound lesson.

I'll give you an example...

Parenting Love

Chrissy was frustrated and annoyed with her thirteen-year-old daughter. She was tired of receiving phone calls from the school about her skipping classes. She never saw her at home since she was always at her friend's house spending the night, and all the back talk was disrespectful and cheeky. The fights were more and more frequent, and the yelling was negatively affecting the siblings. Everyone was done.

As Chrissy listed off the escalated behaviors that had recently shown up in the last five or six months, I mentioned that it sounded like her daughter was hemorrhaging. She was in the midst of a major crisis, and her whole system was in fight-or-flight mode. Recognizing that her daughter was in serious pain (and not just an annoying teenager) shifted the energy. Her psychological injuries were unseen, but the behavioral messages were loud and clear. Chrissy reconsidered her approach with her daughter. With renewed tenderness and compassion, knowing her daughter was suffering, she reached out with love. Her daughter's response was hesitant at first, but then she collapsed into her mom. She shared that she had had some negative interactions with her boyfriend the previous summer, but she hadn't been able to find the words to discuss it or even know if it was okay that she wasn't okay. The situation had overwhelmed her underdeveloped system, and it went into survival mode.

Interestingly enough, softening her dynamic with her daughter allowed Chrissy to be gentler with herself, too. She realized that she was running on mostly empty and had very little emotional capital for her family, let alone herself. As a single mother, she was tapped out but assumed she had to do everything on her own to show her kids what it meant to be strong and independent. As we discussed, being true to herself can include inviting people along in her parenting, expanding her support circle, and accessing resources. She reconnected with her brother, who was also raising teenagers, signed up for parenting classes at the local community center, and refocused her energy on staying connected with her girlfriends and support group. The paradigm shift was profound. The mother and daughter grew individually and collectively as they discovered personal healing and strength, all while staying grounded in their mother-daughter relationship. It was a beautiful transformation of love.

Reset Your System First

As caregivers, parents are on the front line of adolescent cycling emotions and escalated behaviors. You are their witness, the ultimate validation, and support. One of the major paradoxes of life is realizing that, as a parent, putting yourself first is the best thing for your teen. You have to rest your system and take care of your own emotional and physical health, so when you engage with them, you aren't triggered and explode back. We model for our teenagers how to take ourselves seriously by taking care of ourselves, balanced with staying grounded in friendships with family and friends. You need your village of people to support you.

Our kids are watching us all the time and are tuned into our moods and mysteries. We offer them the language and accompanying tools to teach and inform them on how to best navigate life, fully equipped with what they need to not just survive but also thrive. In all sincerity, the best way to love them is to love ourselves first. You are ground zero for them, wherein their survival is anchored, and they learn to trust themselves and grow into the fabulous human beings that they are.

Janey Komm has been a psychotherapist in private practice for over twenty years. She specializes in working with couples, parents, and families to discover a healthy balance between the needs of the individual and the family. Her book, *Nature & Nurture*, offers readers of all ages an informative and transformative experience. She is passionate about sharing the knowledge and tools that will help readers navigate the simplexities of relationships. We simply need to be grounded in ourselves and, at the same time, appreciate and understand the complexities of relationships. She lives in Vancouver, BC, with her husband and three children. For more information, check out her website by scanning the QR code below.

HOME AS A SANCTUARY, NOT A SECOND JOB: THE SOMATIC PATH TO A PEACEFUL HOME

Vikki Fuhrman

To be honest, the prospect of motherhood terrified me. I looked at my withering houseplants and wondered: was this a preview of the parent I would be? Haunted by the ghosts of my own childhood memories, I was paralyzed by the fear that I couldn't provide a perfect life for my children. "Seasoned" mothers only added to the weight, their grim warnings about the "awful" teen years landing like a heavy, familiar dread, as if my own body weren't already "keeping the score" of those formative early adult years.

Every parenting stage can feel like a trap when we believe that "fixing" the outside world will make our child perfect. When we hunt for the right reward-punishment style or use fear to stop a behavior, we are often just trying to quiet our own internal tension and racing heart. This "bottom-up" pressure comes at a high cost: it prevents your teen from learning to listen to their inner cues and navigate life with genuine, embodied confidence.

Now that you've reached these later years, your teen is highly attuned to the energy in the room. If you respond to them from a place of your own unprocessed stress—seeking your own relief rather than their connection—their survival instincts will ignite. This creates a clash of nervous systems, where their need for autonomy meets your need for comfort, resulting in "fireworks" that signal a deep, physical disconnection.

Tending the Inner Landscape

I know the gut-wrenching wait, listening for the rumble of tires scraping the curb that tells me they're safely home, well after curfew, only to be triggered by rage. I know the phone ringer set to full volume all night, just in case—even now that they don't live at home. And I know the two-a.m. ruminating: wondering what they'll make of themselves if they drop out of school or decide not to go to college.

Knowing how to make sense of my internal signals allows me to communicate authentically and calmly. This establishes a trusting and loving bond regardless of how imperfect the environment is. I don't take it for granted when they ask our take on chaotic current events, financial advice, or a gut-check on big decisions. Tending to my own inner landscape allows me to soften the physical grip of "what if" and release the urge to future-trip on what hasn't happened yet. By quieting my internal static, I've traded that old, inherited anxiety for the joy of being a steady witness to their journey. I get to savor the "gold" of the present: the quiet, visceral thrill of watching them navigate obstacles and seeing a genuine self-trust take root in their own bodies.

The Three Pillars of Inner Authority

The most powerful thing you can do for your teen isn't about managing their choices; it's about mastering your own internal signals. When you can discern the data your body is giving you, you can move out of "reaction mode" and into a state of calm presence. This is what I call your Inner Authority.

This is less about a destination and more about how you are showing up, built on three nonlinear pillars. We move through them fluidly at any given time to stay grounded and anchored. This fluid movement is the heart of Somatic Practice—the art of listening to your living body as you navigate the chaos of parenting from the inside out.

1. **Settling the physical self:** This is the skill of reading your internal sensations and releasing the "old history" stored as chronic tension in your muscles. Through a somatic body scan, you learn to track where your body is bracing—a tight jaw, a constricted chest, or a knotted stomach. By simply acknowledging these sensations, you allow the tension to soften, helping your nervous system feel safe and "at home" even when the house is chaotic.

2. **Finding energetic flow:** This is the skill of harmonizing your internal energy by listening to how your body responds to

the outside world. Instead of getting swept up in a story or an "inner dialogue" about your teen's behavior, you tune into the felt sense of the emotion—the heat of anger or the cold prickle of fear. By witnessing these visceral signals without judgment, you allow the energy to flow through you rather than becoming a "firework" in the home. This somatic release is what clears the "fog" of your reactive thoughts, allowing you to regain the mental clarity needed to see the situation—and your child—with fresh eyes.

3. **Integrating mind and body through co-creation:** This is the bridge where your internal stability meets the outside world. By linking your thoughts to a grounded sensation in your body, you access a deeper source of wisdom that allows for true co-creation. This is where you blend your own needs with those of your teen, building a shared foundation built on mutual respect. More importantly, this is the moment you step into a better version of yourself—no longer reacting from the ghosts of your past but responding from the strength of your present.

You and your teen are dynamic and constantly evolving. You need a practice that grows with you. Somatics, fundamentally, moves inner authority from a mental concept into a lived, physical experience.

Somatics practice isn't just a parenting technique; it's a way of living. You are retraining your body to remain grounded, resilient, and present. And that may be the most powerful gift you can offer your teenager.

The Real Test for Me: Chaos Versus Inner Knowing

Years before my oldest son, Hunter, became the college student he is today, I learned to trust my inner knowing through his early childhood challenges. My relationship with his father, which began when we were both teenagers, ended traumatically. I had to transform my life as a single mother of two small boys, eventually fighting for a dyslexia diagnosis that the school system dismissed for years.

Those exhausting years of advocating for my son while anchoring in my own authority became my training ground for somatic practice. They taught me that a parent's inner work isn't separate from the child's well-being—it's the foundation of it. The principles I forged then aren't just personal; they are universal. This is why, when I work with families today, I listen for more than just the facts; I listen for the "inner knowing" that often gets drowned out by external experts.

One family's story stands out....

A Mother's Refusal to Stop Listening

The daughter, a vibrant high school athlete, was sidelined by debilitating back pain after a sports injury. Our medical system is incredibly effective at structural repair—diagnosing specific malfunctions and providing immediate, life-saving interventions like surgery or medication. However, when those tools have done their job and pain persists, it suggests we've moved beyond a "broken part" and into a "protective pattern." In these cases, we need a different approach that focuses on retraining the nervous system's response rather than just treating the symptom. As appointments piled up, the physical density of stress in their home became overwhelming. When specialists suggested the pain might be psychosomatic, they were touching on a vital truth but were unable to be the bridge: her body wasn't "broken," it was simply maintaining a protective survival response that short medical visits aren't yet able to address within our current medical structure.

Fortunately, her mother's own somatic settling anchored in her own internal compass. Deeply attuned to her daughter's unspoken cues, she sensed that the standard "management" plan—while technically sound—was missing the daughter's lived, felt experience. Guided by this visceral knowing, she sought to expand their care team, looking for a path that honored both the physical injury and the body's somatic intelligence.

Through the holistic lens of somatics, the daughter began to explore the profound connection between her emotional distress and her physical pain. She began reworking the memory of her injury, tending not just to the structural trauma, but to the grief of losing her identity as a college-bound athlete. As the emotional tension was acknowledged and released, the physical pain followed suit. This young woman was finally able to return to the classroom and her new, active life, fully integrated.

This journey validated what the mother had sensed all along: healing is most effective when we pair the precision of medical science with the body's innate capacity to be seen, heard, and somatically restored.

The Pay-off: A Secure Connection

Today, my phone rings; it's Hunter. He's calling to talk through a big move, trading his studio for an apartment with a friend.

As I listen, I flash back to his high school years: the countless conversations about dropping out and his insistence on finding his "own" way outside the bureaucracy. Those weren't easy times, but navigating those difficulties—including the years spent learning to advocate for his own needs with dyslexia—taught him the exact skills he needed to trust himself. I realize now that when we, as parents, learn to manage the energy flow of our own nervous systems, we stop riding the roller coaster with our kids. We become the steady ground they land on.

These were messy years, full of doubt and teenage angst. But through the static, our message remained consistent: *What does your gut tell you?* We prioritized his inner knowing over external expectations, even when our own bodies hummed with the urge to step in and take control.

Back on the phone, Hunter lays out the logistics—the costs, the social benefits, the trade-offs. I ask him one simple question: "It sounds like you've thought this through. Do you feel certain about this decision?"

"I know you trust my decision-making," he says, his voice calm and sure. "But I value your opinion. I'd really like to know what you think about this move."

His question isn't a request for validation; it's a desire for connection and shared wisdom. It is the ultimate sign of a secure relationship. He has developed his own Inner Authority, and because he trusts himself first, he finally has the space to trust me, too.

The Legacy We Build

That simple phone call represents something essential: our most powerful tool as parents is our own embodied self-trust. By learning to listen to our body's signals—the gut feelings, the tension, and the quiet knowing—we aren't just navigating today's challenges; we are mirroring for our children how to do the same. This work is about more than solving a teenager's problem. It's about building a living legacy of somatic intelligence and unwavering self-trust for the next generation. It's time to start listening to the wisdom already within you. It's time to trust yourself first.

Vikki Fuhrman, founder of The Bodyology Clinic, is a Somatic Educator who traded the "gut-wrenching wait" of parenting for a grounded Inner Authority. Through her 3-pillar framework—Settling, Flowing, and Co-Creating—she helps high-achieving women move from hyper-vigilance into a somatic state of peace. Vikki believes a peaceful home isn't built on more to-dos, but on the embodied presence that transforms your home from a second job into a sanctuary. Ready to trade the chaos for a stable foundation? What is your body trying to tell you right now? Find out in the free quiz and download your somatic guide, *Home as a Sanctuary*, by scanning the code below.

16

PARENTS DO WELL IF THEY CAN

Jayde Schmutter

——

Hello, survival mode. Hello, short fuse.

When you become a parent, your children become your central focus – often to the exclusion of self-reflection, awareness, and care.

My experience was no different, but when I began to focus on my own emotional well-being and behavior first, things took a turn for the better. This was the missing piece. The difference between just surviving and thriving as a whole family. It transformed how I was able to show up for my children and how they respond to our interactions. In difficult moments, I now try to pause first, check in with myself, and handle my own stress and frustration, so I can respond in a way that fosters connection and improves the relationship.

Emotional Regulation

Emotional regulation is the foundation of every healthy parent-child relationship. Studies have shown a strong link between family dynamics and children's emotional regulation.[5] Regulating emotions is also linked to greater well-being, higher earning potential,[6] and better social interactions.[7]

We all experience moments of overwhelm or dysregulation. When a parent or child is dysregulated, connection breaks down.

When we're dysregulated, we lose access to the thinking part of our brain (the part that lets us pause, assess, and respond in line with our values and intentions). Instead, our nervous system takes over. We react before we can intervene. It happens fast, and we don't realize until after the damage is done.

Does any of this sound familiar? Chances are you've had moments you later wished you'd handled differently. You are, after all, only human. It might mean you lose control of your temper (and yell, argue, threaten, or punish), feel overwhelmed (and withdraw, or seek alone time), feel paralyzed (and shut down, or space out), or struggle to say "no" (the classic people-pleaser).

When your teen ignores you, rolls their eyes, says "whatever" or "I don't care", it's natural to feel disrespected, raise your voice, or repeat the same power struggles you experienced growing up.

The hardest part of all is resisting the natural urge to match their intensity.

A common mistake is trying to teach during a tornado. When they're dysregulated, they can't learn. Lower your voice, slow the pace. That helps their nervous system regulate.

In the moment, ask yourself: Do I want connection or do I want to be right? If you're seeking connection, teach later.

When stress, fatigue, or old patterns take over, it's not about failing; it's about capacity. Burnout, not character, predicts harsh discipline behavior.[8]

Good intentions alone don't change your reactions. Knowing what to do only helps if you can pause first and reset your nervous system, so you're calm enough to apply it.

The good news: once you identify your triggers, your warning signs, and your calming tools, what feels chaotic becomes more predictable and manageable.

Sensitivities, Triggers, and Tolerance

Everyone has a tolerance or threshold for frustration. Some people are more sensitive and have a lower threshold than others. If this threshold is reached, emotions boil over. By reducing exposure to triggers, you lower the baseline stress levels (water in the pot). This means you have a greater tolerance for stressors without losing control.

We all have different triggers. What barely registers for one person can overwhelm another. Triggers are also cumulative, so although it may appear like your child goes from 0-100 in seconds, this is because these triggers can go undetected and unresolved until they boil over. Understanding your specific triggers and warning signs, not just your child's, is where the magic happens.

Connection vs Control

In both my clinical work and my own home, I've seen the same pattern: when parents lead with control (threats, punishment, power struggles), they get momentary compliance at best and defiance at worst. When they lead with connection (presence, curiosity, repair), they get lasting impact. Children internalize what we model. If I want my children to regulate, I have to show them what regulation looks like, especially in the moments when it's hardest.

Emotional regulation and executive functioning are skills. They need to be taught and scaffolded, not punished. Children's brains aren't fully developed until roughly age twenty-five, which means these skills need support far longer than most parents expect. For neurodivergent children, this is even more true. They don't need more judgment. They need more help.

The framing you use is pivotal. Labels like "bad" or "defiant" imply unwillingness—leading to judgment and punishment. "Struggling" or "having difficulty" imply inability and foster compassion and curiosity—prompting education. An effective leader teaches someone who is still learning.

If your child ignores you when it's time to get out of the pool, a controlling reaction would be: "I said NOW... if you don't come this second, we are never going back in the pool again." A calm response would be calmly walking over, taking their hand, and saying, "This was so much fun—it's time to get out for now. Let's get ready... you get to choose the movie for tonight."

Address the Cause, Not the Symptoms

All behavior is communication. When children can't communicate their needs (because they lack awareness or because they don't feel safe enough to express them), they become dysregulated. When a child acts out, they're communicating something they can't yet put into words: an unmet need, frustration they can't tolerate, a problem they can't solve.

They are having a hard time, not giving you a hard time. Our job is to understand, acknowledge, and help them build those skills.

When undesirable behavior repeats, it's important to examine what happens before it.

Awareness allows you to pause and provides choice.

Pause. Regulate. Teach.

In my personal and professional life, I have noticed that emotional dysregulation creates disharmony, conflict, and disengagement—unless I use these moments as opportunities to regulate together (co-regulate) and support calm. The key is to stay regulated when children "explode," model regulation, and co-regulate. I discovered my own triggers, warning signs, and calming tools, and now use these to regulate myself before responding. This can work two-fold through another neuroscience finding called the Neuro-echo effect, in which people mirror your microbehaviors. If your body posture, emotions, and voice are calm, it not only helps calm your nervous system but also theirs. Movement, posture, and breathing help me stay calm enough to respond from a place of understanding and love, rather than react.

For my eldest son, it's a relaxing shower while warm water rains down on him, tickles, massages, an icepack on his head, or chewing ice cubes.

For my youngest, it's pretending to breathe out fire like a dragon together, stomping like a dinosaur, and shaking his worries away.

It's just as important to practice these calming tools outside of the difficult moments. This helps lower your baseline stress, build a buffer for challenging times, and makes it easier to draw on these skills when you really need them.

Emotional Tornado

My son and I are similar in many ways, and while this should make it easier to empathize and connect, it also makes it harder. We both struggle to regulate our emotions, so we don't always respond the way we'd like.

In my family, we are no strangers to feeling overwhelmed. It's natural to revert to traditional discipline, consequences, control—the way I was parented. This only ever seems to lead to power struggles, guilt, shame, regrets, and a relationship in need of repair.

As a psychologist and a mother grieving the motherhood, I made it my mission to find a better way for my kids and for myself.

This led me to develop the ESO framework, a set of simple, practical strategies to help build greater awareness, a calmer home, and a stronger connection.

Emotional and Sensory Overwhelm: 5 Steps to Better Relationships and a Calmer Home

Run through these steps for yourself first, then your child. Once you're familiar with the process, you'll both be equipped to better handle life's daily stressors – now and into the future.

1. Identify triggers for dysregulation and overwhelm.

These might include noise, mess, hunger, fatigue, overscheduling, hormones, rejection, feeling controlled, or conflict. Be specific to you.

2. Manage triggers to reduce overwhelm.

Once you know your triggers, reduce exposure where you can. This might mean stepping away, lowering the lights, putting on music, or building in movement before a transition you know will be hard.

3. Recognise warning signs.

What happens in your body just before you lose it? A tight jaw, shallow breathing, heat rising in your chest? Learn those signals. They're your early warning system.

4. Find your calming tools.

Build a personal toolkit of what actually works for you in the thick of it. Brain and body resets. For me, it's movement (muscle workouts, stretching, or open-chest calm dominance posture) and breathing (a long exhale with a hand on my chest or stomach). For you, it might be cold water on your face (dive reflex), humming, or naming the feeling "I'm feeling frustrated right now" (affect labeling). Experiment and keep what helps you.

5. Document your ESO Plan (for yourself and your child).

Write it down. Keep it where you can find it when you need it most— not when you're calm, but when you're about to lose it. Put it on the fridge, on your phone, on the bathroom wall. Adjust as you learn what works.

"I can't let them get away with poor behavior."

Keep doing what you've always done, and you'll keep getting the same outcome.

Staying calm with your child isn't being soft or weak. You're demonstrating the strength and courage to choose connection over control, even when it's hard.

You are being a leader instead of a drill sergeant.

You don't need to yell to be taken seriously; be mean to teach a lesson; or have your children fear you to do as you ask.

Connection isn't letting them off the hook. You can be kind and still hold the boundary.

Shift the story from "They're being difficult" to (a curiosity about why) "They're dysregulated" or "struggling." This understanding/compassion lowers defensiveness. Reframing like this changes the tone and the outcome, leading to lessons that land.

Calm leadership is powerful enough. You simply need to be calm, clear, and consistent about expectations or boundaries.

For example: When navigating difficult transitions, preempt the response, set up clear expectations at the outset, and get their buy-in. "We are going to play this video game for 20 minutes, and when I say time is up, you are going to hand back the remotes—no arguments, and no fights. Okay?" Provide praise when they follow through. And if they struggle at first, remind them of your arrangement, then offer praise after they act in line with it. Don't reward them for ignoring you by giving them more time. I've observed improved cooperation and less resistance.

No Time. No Energy. Too Busy. It Won't Work.

Would you take the chance?

A few simple shifts can be all it takes to gain momentum.

Even small moments of calm connection strengthen your child's brain and your relationship.

Knowing why reactions happen and how to recognize them opens space for change.

You're not failing. You're doing your best. You just need a different toolkit—one that works for you and your child. You're learning and making progress, even when it's hard. Progress is rarely linear. It will be more like a dance—two steps forward, one step back, two to the side, and another one forward.

Remember to prioritize your own well-being and self-compassion, and to know your limits. This is not selfish; it's necessary.

By helping yourself, you are helping your child. It's the equivalent of putting on your oxygen mask on a plane before tending to your child.

When parents do well, kids do too.

Jayde Schmutter is a psychologist and mother of two based in Sydney, Australia. Over the past 20 years, she has supported thousands of children, teens, and adults in learning, connecting, and thriving. Her work spans children's hospitals, children's sport, and social services, delivering assessments, counselling, coaching, workshops, research, and consulting. Combining professional expertise with lived parenting experience, Jayde is passionate about helping families flourish through greater awareness, compassion, and connected relationships. As founder of NeuroBright, she empowers parents and educators with practical strategies to create calmer, more supportive homes and classrooms. To access your free ESO guide, scan the code below.

SOMEONE TO COME BACK TO

Sue Ellen Sweeney

Alone in a small garage apartment near my daughters' high school, I went through a difficult time. My life had fallen apart. I was told not to attend my teenage daughters' events. Cut off from family finances and dealing with a broken foot, I felt anxious about how I would support myself. The days all felt the same, full of tears, prayers, and searching for comfort under the afghan my grandmother made for me.

During this lonely time, I kept asking myself, *Who am I?* I examined my life decisions.

As our children grew up and left home, communication with my husband had broken down, and our marriage suffered. I felt unseen and unheard in the family I had spent years caring for.

The heart-wrenching decision to leave my husband left my six children, including three teenage daughters, confused, angry, and hurt, leading them to distance themselves from me. They refused to speak with me, and my youngest daughter said, "I am not going to speak with you until you do what Dad is telling you to do."

Without their love and connection, I felt I had lost not only my family but also my sense of purpose and direction. Physically and emotionally immobilized, I watched raindrops slide down the window, and squirrels pilfer food from the birdfeeder, feeling as though I, too, was stuck, unable to move forward.

How could I continue? There seemed to be no path forward, and I had no idea how to connect with my children.

A turning point arrived with my lawyer's poignant words: "You can stay curled up in that garage apartment watching your children drive by, *or* you can take care of yourself so when they're ready to come back, they have someone to come back to."

This message was a beacon of hope, albeit overwhelming. It was the catalyst I needed to begin a journey of self-discovery and healing.

I realized that to be the parent my teens truly needed, I had to be emotionally present and mentally healthy. This insight was confirmed in my work with teens as a mental health RN in psychiatric settings and in the community.

For parents of teens, the challenge often lies in navigating the delicate balance between guiding our children and allowing them the space to grow. The solution begins with self-care and open communication. By prioritizing our well-being and embracing our authentic selves, we set a powerful example for our children and become more available to them, providing a safe space for them to learn and grow.

It is essential to foster an environment that encourages open dialogue and nurtures emotional connections.

I had failed. I struggled with how to repair what had gone so wrong. In the hustle of family and career, I had lost myself, feeling noble in my self-sacrifice and striving to meet others' expectations. Realizing that my relentless pursuit of perfection as a wife and mother was a pattern I learned from my own parents and subconsciously repeated, and that it had led me away from being the parent I wanted to be, was a revelation. I chose to do what I needed to do to repair relationships and connect with my six children. I believe repair is always possible!

As a school and psychiatric nurse, and now a transformational and Positive Intelligence family coach, I've learned that the most crucial gift we can offer our teens is our presence—emotionally available and mentally balanced. Nurturing our own well-being can transform our relationships with our children, guiding them through their own journeys with love and understanding.

I have also learned just how important parents are to children, including teens who may be giving messages to the contrary. Do not believe that you are not important to your teen! This is not true! A story that really brings this home is what I heard from a 12-year-old boy during a group gratitude exercise on a psychiatric inpatient unit. This boy was seen as "unmanageable" by his parents and by several foster placements he had lived in, not "placeable" by the social service system. His response to the question, "What are you most grateful for?" was "my family."

By working with teens and parents in these settings, I have seen parents who really do not know how to manage or connect with their tween and teen rely on the professionals to somehow transform their child. While I am in total agreement that a higher level of support is sometimes necessary for the well-being of the child and for critical psychiatric care, I believe that the strengthening of the parent-child relationship is the best strategy for mental health. Parents often don't get the support needed to build relationships and create an environment where all in the family can thrive.

My personal transformation led me to recognize and highlight the critical importance of emotional presence and mental health in parenting. I understood that my fears and insecurities had inadvertently created a barrier between my children and me, sabotaging our relationship.

Growing up as a pleaser, I was driven by a fear of failure instilled by achievement-focused parents. If I came home with a high grade, the question would be, "Did anyone score higher?" Conversations often centered around achievement and comparisons. Despite my vow to parent differently, I subconsciously repeated these patterns, focusing on external success and neglecting my children's emotional needs. Even with a background in nursing and a graduate degree in family development, I found myself echoing my parents' mindset, as illustrated when I asked my son's English teacher how he could improve his 92% score. My son's response spelled discouragement.

Through self-reflection, I also realized I believed I needed to control everything as a parent, thinking I was the expert responsible for ensuring everything ran smoothly. My tendency to please others maintained a supportive relational environment but avoided challenges. I did not know how to manage conflict. When my marriage ended, and my children became distant, I was forced to examine *why* they were reluctant to connect with me.

Reflecting on my daughter's story as she shared it with me in an open conversation during the repair stage of our relationship was particularly poignant. During her teenage years, she often retreated to her room when upset, hoping someone would notice her distress and reach out to her. She longed for a conversation, but instead felt isolated. Hearing this, I realized I had repeated my parents' pattern of avoiding conflict, leaving her to navigate her emotions alone.

My son's story was equally eye-opening. Years after leaving home, he revealed that my visible fear of potential pitfalls like substance abuse had pushed him toward those behaviors. In his teenage years, he experimented with substances and skipped school, reacting to the pressure he sensed from me. This revelation filled me with regret and sorrow, highlighting how my unmanaged emotions had hindered my ability to connect with him.

These stories were even more motivation to continue doing my inner work. They underscored the need for me to confront my fears and learn to manage my emotions effectively. Through my inner work, I began having open conversations with my children, acknowledging my past mistakes and expressing my commitment to change. I listened more, spoke less, and created a safe space for them to share their thoughts without fear of judgment.

This transformation allowed me to rebuild trust and understanding with my children. Being a present and mentally healthy parent is about being willing to grow and change alongside them. I celebrate my evolving relationships with my now adult children.

As a coach, I aim to help parents avoid the pitfalls I faced, which left my teens without the necessary support, and help them create healthy, connecting relationships. One client transformed her experience of living in chaos in a failing marriage to confidently co-parenting with a partner who was struggling with addiction, becoming the parent her children needed.

A recent client facing mental health challenges learned to shift her thinking patterns that were sabotaging her happiness and career. After three months of Positive Intelligence coaching, she gained tools to overcome hyper-vigilance, decrease her anxiety, and improve relationships with her husband and teen.

The Positive Intelligence system, developed by Shirzad Chamine, helps identify mental patterns that hinder happiness and success. Through coaching and community, clients gain tools and support to re-pattern their thinking and achieve desired life outcomes. Learning this system and practicing it daily continues to provide powerful tools and support for myself and the clients who have embraced it.

Positive Intelligence is a mental fitness practice. Here are the simple steps that have been researched to be powerful in so many lives:

- **Identify Your Saboteurs:** Recognize the negative voices in your head that sabotage your success and happiness. These are the self-defeating thoughts and behaviors that hold you back.

- **Strengthen Your Sage:** Develop the positive part of your mind, which is your inner Sage. This involves cultivating qualities like empathy, curiosity, creativity, and calm, clear-headed focus.

- **PQ Reps:** Practice simple mental exercises called PQ (Positive Intelligence Quotient) reps. These exercises help you shift from negative to positive thinking by focusing on your senses and being present in the moment.

- **Intercept Saboteurs:** Learn techniques to stop your Saboteurs in their tracks. This involves recognizing when they appear and using specific strategies to weaken their influence.

- **Build Mental Muscles:** Practice these steps continuously to build your mental muscles. This helps you respond to life's challenges with a positive mindset and resilience.

By following these steps, you can enhance your mental fitness and create more happiness and success in your family life and your career.

You might think that you don't have the time to learn and integrate this practice into your daily life. However, the beauty of Shirzad Chamine's Positive Intelligence practice lies in its brief, efficient exercises, designed to fit seamlessly into daily routines such as commuting or taking breaks. By incorporating PQ reps into everyday activities, you prioritize mental fitness, which not only enhances productivity and efficiency but also improves work-life balance. The program's flexibility ensures it can accommodate any schedule, demonstrating that even a few minutes a day can lead to significant benefits over time.

You can break free from inherited patterns of achievement-focused, controlling parenting and, instead, foster genuine connections by recognizing and overcoming negative thought patterns using this system.

I encourage you to embrace the JOY of guiding your teen in their development while experiencing the benefits of growing with them through all the changes and challenges this stage of life brings.

Doing your inner work requires support. It would be my honor and privilege to be your guide in your journey. Together, we can break free from unproductive patterns and guide our children with love and empathy. The rewards of doing your inner work are invaluable and worth the effort.

Sue Ellen Sweeney, a transformational Positive Intelligence coach, helps families transform stress into joy through mental fitness. As a mother of six and grandmother of 12, she values family time and nature. Guided by faith, Sue is committed to fostering connected, loving relationships and supporting others in achieving this dream. With over 30 years as an RN specializing in children and families, she brings extensive experience. Discover your mental patterns with a free Saboteur Assessment at https://www.sueellen.live/ or schedule a consultation to explore your unique needs.

LIGHTHOUSE PARENTING: A JOURNEY OF AWARENESS AND PRESENCE

Sally Bennett

Tired.

Overwhelmed.

Burnt out.

I didn't know it then, but that exhaustion was my body's way of calling time-out and asking a quiet question: *Who am I underneath all the roles? Mother. Wife. Teacher. Regulator of everyone else's emotions.*

Finding the answer opened the way to travel. It was the moment I stopped believing that time out meant abandoning my family. In saying yes to a meditation conference, I realized I was no longer abandoning myself.

I packed my suitcase and went.

When my suitcase didn't arrive at baggage claim upon my return home, I surprised myself by smiling. It felt like the universe's way of confirming what I'd released during the conference. Lifetimes of pain no longer needed to be carried.

That day, I sighed, feeling my smile widen as I lightly stepped onto my train home with only my hand luggage. Inside it were just a few essentials, the gifts this journey had gently placed in my care: wisdom, softness, self-trust, and the quiet practice of befriending myself.

When the Lighthouse Goes Dark

As my train carried me home, my thoughts traveled back to the COVID years, a series of losses that quietly reshaped my nervous system. I lost my sister to brain cancer. I said goodbye to my mother with dementia. My two eldest withdrew from my life once again. And my fur child, whose toy bear had once been perfectly placed on the hallway floor for all to trip over, ventured onto the highway and did not return.

So, during COVID, we filled our home again with the wagging joy of not one, but two tails. The adventures continued; though, having already been emotionally knocked off my feet, I was now also physically knocked down by our playful pups, breaking three bones in my left leg. Taking ten months to learn to walk again, I noticed how lost I had become.

I had spent years just surviving. And while I was surviving, my youngest children had grown into teenagers. I had missed the transition, and now I was trying to parent them from empty. My boys, just two years apart, had stopped talking to each other. They lived side by side but in separate worlds. I didn't have the energy to fix it. I longed for the simplicity of my own 70's and 80's childhood for them.

What kept me moving through those years were my roles: Mother. Wife. Worker.

Still, I felt buried in the generational patterns of home and work, navigating a parental landscape we were never prepared for. There I was trying to regulate screen-shaped teenagers while learning to steady myself.

Although my world hadn't changed, I had. In seven days of meditation, I had remembered who I was, and a spark of truth had been ignited as I recalled a conversation with my youngest: "Mum, don't give me the story that you were once a child and you understand what I'm going through; you were never a child during COVID." True.

And from that place, the world, my family, could be met differently. I wasn't fixing or managing anymore. I was walking forward, lighter, along a road less traveled, yet deeply familiar to my inner being. I began shifting from emotional caregiving and household caretaking to something new.

Packing with the Lighthouse in Mind

My thoughts wandered to the retreat meditation, where an inner message landed like a whisper, yet it carried a sense of direction. *Sometimes the most loving thing you can do for your children is to remember yourself.*

The mindfulness week highlighted a different way to parent teens, shifting from endless, stormy, broken negotiations to a shared invitation: "Let's grow together, and become the best we can be and more!"

I realized that I now needed one more item in my hand luggage: a torchlight.

A phrase came to me, something I'd heard years ago but never understood until now: lighthouse parenting. Like an anchored lighthouse, my role is not to enter the sea, chase the boat, or argue with the storm. Rather, to calm without control, love without rescue, and provide space without withdrawal.

The torch helped me see myself and illuminated what my children were carrying after COVID. Holding this torch showed me how to move beyond my roles and into the rhythm of their teenage world, knowing when to step in, step beside, or, more often than not, simply stand still and breathe.

Shining Light on the Parenting Path

As the train moved up the mountains towards home, my smile deepened. The once-troubling teen years felt like they were gliding away, and, just as at the connecting airport, it was time to shift from parenting children to guiding emerging adults.

In the early years, we parented with co-regulation. In the middle years, with shared calm tools. And now, with teenagers applying parallel regulation, continuing a nightly ritual of turning on the porch light but with a new intention: offering a quiet beacon through the emotional waves of adolescence.

For teenagers, this shift communicates: *I trust your nervous system to learn itself while I remain grounded and present.* I was learning that they don't need us to calm their storm; they need us not to lose ourselves while they discover themselves.

As the train slowed and pulled into the station, I spotted my husband waiting on the platform, ready as always to greet and carry the luggage. Today, there was no luggage to lift, no heavy case filled with overpacked expectations, emotional responsibility, or unspoken strain. What I carried now sat lightly on my shoulder.

In the moment of shifting from the solo traveler to the returned adventurer, there is an excited travel buzz and a soft pause at home. And in this swirl of mixed goodbyes and hellos, I reached into my bag for my take-home notes, written from clarity, not exhaustion.

Journaling helped me understand who I am beneath all the roles and who we are becoming as a family. This note was ready to be discussed and shared on the fridge: a family agreement, including the option that, when emotions run high, anyone can step away. Not to avoid the issue, but to let our nervous systems settle.

Guided through the Storm by Light

And while we can laugh at the small things, we are also learning to smile through the important moments that help us navigate the way. So, knowing that every voyage has its moments, and parenting is no different, here are a few steadying awarenesses to support parallel regulation:

- Know your triggers. Listen to your body messages. These are generational patterns you may no longer choose to carry.

- When teens say, "you're yelling" or "you're over the top," it is often not an accusation. It's dysregulation. Learn new tones and scripts that meet stormy weather with calm.

- Release the habit of carrying others' emotions; regulate beside them, not for them.
- Adjustments for growth require rest and reset time. Nourish yourself daily; eat, play, love, and laugh in small sustainable ways.

And so, as we drove through the garden gates of home, I took a slow breath and allowed the answer to rise: Who am I?

I am my suitcase, my day pack, my handbag, my empty pockets, and my filled pockets. I'm everything I choose to be and choose not to be... I now travel the day lightly, with a greater awareness of self-love. Presence, not rescue. Care, not carrying. Connection, not responsibility.

Looking back, that journey was far more than a spiritual retreat or a pause from life. And something surprising happened.

My family survived without me.

In fact, my absence, particularly my mothering presence, created space. Space for freedom and growth choices. Space for a bachelor pantry and questionable meal decisions, space for natural responsibility and consequences of no one pressing start on the dishwasher. Space for independence and the understanding that socks do not walk themselves to the washing machine. Space for everyone to find their own rhythm with the quiet awareness that their rooms do not magically tidy themselves.

Traveling Together

The greatest outcome of this parenting shift was not something I envisaged creating, yet it unfolded naturally over the months after my return. My once-living side-by-side teenage boys found their way back to reconnect.

You see, the emotional terrain I had been traveling for years had quietly mirrored itself in their brotherly distance. My own fatigue had shaped the family weather of our home. And when I stopped abandoning myself and shifted how I cared as a parent, the atmosphere softened—so did the space between them.

Our nightly ritual of turning on the porch light reminded me of the streetlights in my childhood. A steady, constant signal that said, 'home is safe, connection is here.' In this family lighthouse approach, shared moments resurfaced, laughter returned, and brotherhood remembered its own rhythm of friendship.

I hadn't tried to fix anything. We simply stayed present. Shining a steady light.

And that was enough.

Sally Bennett is a mother of four in a happy second marriage who enjoys simplifying parenting research to support families. She draws on over 25 years of experience in both parenting and teaching, with a master's degree in education counseling, Children's Yoga Therapy Teacher, author/illustrator, and educational consultant—helping families and classrooms navigate big emotions with presence, connection, and joy. Connect with her on Facebook at The Conscious Calm Parent to access her Teenage Family Agreements, mindful communication scripts for connecting with neurotypical & neurodiverse teenagers, and practical tools for parallel regulation and strengthening self-worth.

EVERYTHING IS FINE: LET THE SHIFT HAPPEN

Vibha Arora, MS, MFT

———

It's a typical Thursday afternoon, and you're doing your transportation duty — driving your teen to practice. At yet another red light, you glance over at them. Their face is buried in their phone, but somehow you can still see the preschool version of them. The nonstop chatterbox. The one who once narrated every thought and every sight seen out loud.

And suddenly, you have a realization. This stage of parenting is hard. Not bad hard — just very different hard.

And you're so right.

You begin to wonder if the one-word answers, the grunts, eye rolls, and slammed doors mean you're not doing very well at this whole parenting thing.

And you're wrong.

What you're witnessing is exactly what's supposed to be happening. Your child is in the developmental stage of individuation — the process of figuring out who they are and how they want to be in the world. This stage is not a sign of disconnection; it's a sign of growth. It's your invitation to step back and watch this rite of passage unfold.

Ready or not, they're going to keep growing. What *is* within your control is how you show up during this evolution — not only in the relationship with them, but in your own opportunities to grow alongside them.

When Parenting Changes

Parenting during the tween and teen years goes through a major transformation. We are invited — or perhaps demanded — to shift from managing behavior to mentoring autonomy. We move from director to guide. Instead of giving answers, we begin asking questions that help them find their own answers. This shift is profound — both for them and for us.

In these years, the parenting dance becomes one of letting go while staying connected. We're asked to witness transformation instead of trying to control it. And that is no small ask.

After working with hundreds of parents, one thing is clear: this rapid shift from the younger childhood years into adolescence often brings parents to feelings of uncertainty, grief, and self-doubt. Many parents quietly wonder if they'll ever be cool enough, smart enough, or good enough to truly connect with their child again.

They used to adore us. Now we wonder if they even like us.

If this sounds familiar, you're not alone. Welcome to parenting a teen.

It's Not Them – It's Us

As counterintuitive as it may sound, parenting at this stage has less to do with our children and more to do with us. We're being asked to do less for them — less fixing, less rescuing, and far less attempting to control their behavior. At the same time, we're invited to turn inward. More awareness about what activates us. More practice regulating our own nervous systems. And more trust in a process we cannot rush (or slow down).

While the teen years are notorious for behaviors that push our buttons, their behavior isn't actually the hardest part. What's most challenging is learning how to sit in our own discomfort. Perhaps memories from our own adolescence resurface. Maybe fears about their future begin to rise. Or perhaps we're simply coming to terms with the reality that these humans we've been responsible for are slowly becoming responsible for themselves.

The work here is not to eliminate discomfort — but to tolerate it. To stay present while they learn.

As Pulitzer Prize–winning author Barbara Kingsolver once said about parenting: "It's the one job where the better you are, the more surely you won't be needed in the long run." And isn't that what we want? To raise independent, capable, responsible adults.

Paradoxically, this stage — when they crave autonomy — is also the one in which they require deep connection. Our task is to hold both. Not either/or. Both.

When teens pull away, prioritize friends, scroll endlessly on their phones, or retreat into their own worlds, it's easy to take it personally. However, this isn't rejection. It's biology. Their brains are wired to differentiate. This isn't defiance or disrespect — it's developmental. Their job is to become themselves. Our job is to create a safe, nurturing, accepting, and emotionally grounded space for them to do that work — without us placing our unresolved emotions or unhealed stories onto them.

Parenting during this stage can be both messy and magical at the same time. Supporting tweens and teens on their journey toward independence requires conscious awareness, flexibility, and a willingness to allow change. Independence cannot be taught. It must be experienced. And experience includes mistakes — theirs and ours. Missteps will happen in the relationship itself, too. These moments are not failures; they are how we learn.

As a therapist and parent coach, at this point, many parents I've worked with will ask some version of this: *I understand this in theory — but what does it actually look like in real life? How do I stay connected with my emerging adult? And how do I do this without losing my mind?*

Valid questions.

At the heart of this stage are a couple of anchors that can keep you grounded.

The first: *We are raising adults, not children.* An idea Dr. Julie Lythcott-Haims captures beautifully in her book *How to Raise an Adult: Break Free of the Overparenting Trap and Prepare Your Kid for Success.* It's about zooming out: What are the characteristics you hope your child will have when they are 25? What kind of adult will they be—and what kind of relationship with them—are you building toward?

The second anchor comes from parenting expert Dr. Laura Markham and is easy to remember:

QTIP — Quit Taking It Personally

When we stop making our teen's behavior about our own insecurities, then we can create space to respond with clarity rather than reactivity.

Here's what this can look like in real life. Your teen comes home from school extra salty. Clearly, something is bothering them. So you gently ask a crazy question, "How was your day?"

An explosion follows. They exhale loudly, clench their fists, stare through you, and scream, "Why are you always in my business?! Why can't you just leave me alone?!" And then promptly stomp away.

You're human, and so you will have a reaction to their words and behavior. You'll feel it. However, if you remain grounded and committed to remembering to take a breath and pause, you can move from reaction to response. It's okay if it takes many breaths and not just one. There's no emergency here. No rush. What's important is to take the time to get your activated nervous system regulated again. Once you've done that, the response can be as simple as one word: *Ouch.* That's enough. Nothing more is required in that moment.

Ouch creates space between reaction and response. It allows you to model emotional regulation rather than power. You're not allowing disrespect — you're embodying the skills you hope they'll develop. Staying calm. Navigating discomfort. Maintaining connection under stress.

From this space, you can lead with curiosity instead of correction. You can show up with presence instead of power. From here, you can lean into connection and step away from trying to control.

Finally, the question most parents eventually ask, and want/need to know is: *Am I doing this right?*

Success in the teen years looks different. It's not measured by clean rooms, perfect grades, or consistently polite tones and ever-pleasant attitudes. It's quieter — and far more meaningful. Success looks like emotional resilience. Problem-solving skills. Accountability. Kindness. Integrity.

The idea here is not for us to raise children who behave well in our presence. Rather, we are raising adults who can function well in our absence. The world doesn't need more followers running on the hamster wheel of conditioned expectations. It needs grounded humans who can think critically, feel deeply, communicate clearly, and lead with heart.

Everything Is Fine

Parenting during this season invites us to trust the seeds we've already planted — the values, the connection, the love, the goodness.

They're still there. They're simply undergoing a little construction.

It may feel loud and chaotic now, but like every stage of parenting, this one, too, shall pass. Let them go so they can grow. Trust the unfolding.

Here's a little reminder to leave you with: You are doing one of the hardest jobs on the planet—and you are doing it with intention, courage, and heart. Your tween/teen is lucky to have you, even if they don't always show it.

Just remember, in the familiar words of tweens and teens everywhere: *Everything is fine.*

Vibha Arora is a Transformation and Parenting Coach who helps clients look beneath the surface for lasting solutions rather than quick fixes. With a Master's in Marriage and Family Therapy, she's a certified Positive Discipline Facilitator and Conscious Parenting Guide. For over a decade, she has provided a judgment-free space for parents to process challenges and celebrations while learning innovative parenting tools. By combining Positive Discipline and Conscious Parenting, Vibha helps families practice Control Free Parenting for long-term connection. Tune into her podcast, *Kaleidoscope: Shifting Perspectives with a Twist*, and download a free guided reset at vibha-arora.com.

SECTION THREE

HARD MOMENTS, REAL GROWTH

—————

WHEN EMOTIONS RUN HIGH, START WITH THE NERVOUS SYSTEM

Dr. Ann-Louise Lockhart, PsyD, ABPP

Years ago, I was driving to work during one of those blazing hot summers. It was painfully hot. Everything along the roadside was dry. The grass looked like straw, brittle, yellow, and fragile.

A few days later, I drove past the same stretch of road and saw that a patch of grass had caught on fire. The grass was completely charred.

Then the rain came. A torrential downpour.

Days later, I noticed something. Right in the middle of that burned circle, new grass had started to grow. It was bright green, vibrant, and alive. But the grass surrounding it still looked like straw. Pale, dry, and trying to survive.

I remember thinking, *Well, that's interesting.*

The grass was literally burnt to a crisp, and yet the new growth coming up in the middle looked healthier than what was there before.

I didn't know it at the time, but that moment became a metaphor I would return to again and again in my work with families as a pediatric psychologist and a parent coach. I've even used it for myself during hard parenting seasons.

Sometimes what looks like giving up is really a nervous system that's overloaded and needing a reset.

Why It Feels So Hard

As a parent to a tween or teen, there's a good chance you've had moments where you've thought: *Really? Another hard phase? Another struggle? Another fire?*

Maybe you've even whispered to yourself, "Haven't I been through enough? Shouldn't this be easier by now?"

It's not just you. I hear this story often.

In my parent coaching work over the past 20 years, I've met with thousands of parents who are doing the hard work of raising teens while also carrying the weight of their own stories. Sometimes that story includes trauma. Loss. Chronic stress. A medical diagnosis. A childhood where they had to grow up too fast. A history of pain or instability.

It's not just, "My teen is being difficult." It feels like, "I already fought so hard to survive. I want this part to be calmer. Easier."

It might sound like:

"I paid my dues."

"I had a terrible start, so life should be smoother now."

"Parenting my teen should not be taking me out like this."

I get it. I've had those thoughts too.

But what I've learned, both personally and professionally:

Sometimes when parenting feels the hardest, it's not because you're doing it wrong. It might be that your teen's internal world is on fire. Not the kind of fire you can see from the outside. Not the kind you can easily fix with a lecture or a consequence. I'm talking about the kind of fire that happens inside their body.

You know what gives me hope?

Millennial parents are rewriting the script. According to a Lurie Children's survey of 1,000 millennial parents, about 80% say talking with their kids about mental health is *very important*, and 98% report having those conversations, even though two-thirds say their own parents never talked with them about mental health.[9]

I love this! It means we're raising a generation that's more emotionally aware, open, and better equipped to talk about feelings and stress more than many of us ever were. That's incredibly hopeful for our teens' future.

When you're raising a teen who feels everything deeply, learning how to start with the nervous system is part of that new script.

When emotions run high, start with the nervous system. Then you can address the behavior.

Interoception: The Sense You Need to Talk About

Most parents have never heard the word *interoception*. It's not something that comes up in everyday parenting conversations, and it's definitely not something our parents talked to us about.

But once you understand it, it will change how you interpret your teen's behavior.

Interoception is one of our senses. Yes, we have more than five.

Most of us learned about sight, hearing, taste, touch, and smell. But three additional senses are just as important when it comes to stress, emotions, and self-regulation:

- **Proprioception:** awareness of where your body is in space

- **Vestibular:** balance and movement (inner ear)

- **Interoception:** awareness of what's happening inside your body

Interoception is how your brain and body communicate about your internal state. Heartbeat. Breathing. Hunger. Fullness. Pain. Nausea. Tension.

It's also tied to homeostasis, your body's ability to maintain balance and stability. That's why interoception connects to anxiety, panic, overwhelm, emotional shutdown, irritability, and difficulty calming down.

Essentially, interoception is the body's internal messaging system. For many tweens and teens, that system can get extremely loud, or they may misread discomfort as danger. They're still figuring themselves out.

Why "Sense" and "Perception" Aren't the Same

A teen sees their parent walking toward them. That's sensation. Vision. Neutral information.

But their brain might notice mom's quick pace or serious expression and interpret it as, *Oh no. Bro is mad. What did I do now?*

That's perception.

Perception isn't just about what's happening outside. It's shaped by what's happening inside the body.

If the heart is already racing...

If the stomach is tight...

If breathing is shallow...

Then the brain is more likely to interpret neutral things as threatening.

So instead of "Mom is walking toward me," the body and brain say, *Danger. Brace yourself.*

That's why "Sweetie, you're fine" often doesn't register. They're not choosing to be dramatic. Their body is sounding an alarm based on the information they're receiving and getting ready for the fight.

A Pattern I See Over and Over Again

I once worked with London, a 12-year-old whose mom started getting alerts on her smartwatch that her daughter's heart rate was skyrocketing during physical education at school. Sometimes up to 200. London would get dizzy, leave class, end up in the nurse's office, and then go home.

Her mom took her to a cardiologist. The full workup was done. The tests came back normal. London was cleared medically. But the episodes kept happening.

The family started wondering, *if it's not medical, then what is it?*

That's when they met me, a pediatric psychologist trained to make sense of the interaction between physical symptoms and psychological symptoms.

When I met London, I didn't see someone who was "dramatic" or "attention-seeking." I saw a tween whose body was sending intense signals, and whose brain didn't yet know how to interpret those signals accurately.

We talked about interoception.

I explained, "Your body is doing what bodies do during exercise. Heart rate increases. Breathing gets faster. Body temperature heats up."

But because London's attention kept going back to those sensations and interpreting them as dangerous (*What's wrong with me?*), her brain went into protection mode (*I need to do something!*). Fear kicked in. Her body escalated.

When she was allowed to escape (go home), it reinforced the cycle.

Body sensation ¬ fear ¬ more sensation ¬ more fear ¬ escape ¬ repeat.

This is what happens when interoception gets stuck on high volume. Logic can't get through.

Here's what I want you to know as a parent who keeps showing up: Your teen isn't always analyzing the situation (that's logic). Sometimes they're reacting to their body (that's interoception).

That's where I start with my signature Resist-Reset-Rest Approach. Don't ignore behavior. Don't excuse it. No over-reassurance. Stop trying to solve a nervous-system problem with logic and lectures. There is a better way.

The Resist-Reset-Rest Approach

Here's what I teach parents to do when emotions are high and the body is sending loud signals.

Don't focus on fixing your teen. Instead, help their nervous system relax enough for their thinking brain to come back online.

Step 1: Resist the Fight

Lower your voice. Slow your body.

If your teen is escalated, your calm matters more than your words. Speak slower. Move slower. Unclench your jaw. Drop your shoulders.

You are leading the resistance against their attempts to shut down.

Step 2: Reset With One Script

Pick one line and stick with it. Don't give a speech.

"I can tell you're not yourself. Let's try that again."

"We don't have to talk right now. I'm here when you're ready."

"I hear you. I'm still going to hold the limit."

"Your body is on high alert. Let's help it settle first."

"That got big fast. Want a reset and a do-over?"

Step 3: Rest the Body

Name the feeling and connect it to the body.

"You feel nervous when thinking about the test and feel it in your stomach. Let's take a few breaths."

"You were so tense, your shoulders tightened, and you got a headache. Let's tense your shoulders even more, breathe in, and then shake it out."

"You got scared, so your heart started racing. Let's go for a walk."

"You are so angry with your sister and feel heated. Let's grab an ice pack and place it on the back of your neck."

This helps your teen build body awareness and teaches their brain, *This sensation is connected to a feeling, not real danger.*

Common Challenges (and What Helps)

"My teen refuses every strategy."
Focus on your regulation and give space.

"I'm going to step back. I'll check in with you later."

"I try to stay calm, but I get triggered."

Of course you do. When you feel yourself speeding up, say:

"I need a minute, so I don't say this the wrong way."

"What if my teen is being disrespectful?"

You can hold a boundary and still start with regulation.

"I'm willing to talk when you're respectful. Let's reset and try again."

A Success Story

London and her parents practiced this approach. Instead of rescuing her and giving in to her panic, they coached her through the nervous system alert. They said: "We practiced the Resist-Reset-Rest approach for two weeks. Mom chose one script and one reset tool."

By week two, London's heart rate steadily decreased. At times, she still got overwhelmed and pushed back, but recovered faster while developing insight into her body and her reactions. Mom stopped feeling like she had to win the fight. Her perception of London and the situation shifted. They were able to have calm conversations, and London was more receptive to her mom's feedback.

That's the goal: A more balanced teen and healthier parent-teen connections.

The Green Grass Will Come Back

That day on the road, I expected the burned grass to stay burned (not really, but stick with me as I wrap up this metaphor). But life doesn't always work like that. Sometimes the part that looked destroyed becomes the part that grows back the brightest.

If you're struggling right now, it doesn't mean you're doing parenting wrong. If your teen is struggling right now, that's not the end of the story.

When you learn how to understand what's happening under the surface, you stop taking everything personally. You stop fighting every reaction. You stop trying to "fix" them in the moment.

You start helping them come back to themselves.

And yes, the grass can grow back greener.

Dr. Ann-Louise Lockhart is a pediatric psychologist, parent coach, author, national speaker, and mom to two teens who helps parents reduce conflict and build stronger, more connected relationships. She has worked with thousands of families across multiple settings, specializing in ADHD, executive functioning, and anxiety. Dr. Lockhart is the author of *Love the Teen You Have: A Practical Guide to Transforming Conflict Into Connection* and has appeared as a trusted expert on *The Today Show*, *ABC News*, and *CBS Mornings*. She is passionate about helping families lead with curiosity. Scan the QR code to download her free Nervous System Reset guide.

FROM CONTROL TO CONNECTION: HOW TO TAKE YOURSELF FROM REACTING TO RESPONDING IN THE TRIGGERING MOMENTS

Dr. Lynne Maureen Hurdle and Justin Hurdle-Price

How often do we find ourselves facing situations with our children that seem deliberately designed to push our buttons and trigger us? The two of us will explain our perspective from opposite sides of the situational table.

LYNNE: As mother and son, we've lived this and gained wisdom from our successes and mistakes. As a mom of two sons and a conflict coach working with parent groups, I thought I had this parenting thing on lock back then. The truth is, I was failing both of my sons, but most especially Justin. I needed to change, and it was my work with my client Jocelyn that saved me.

Jocelyn had three daughters who each pushed her buttons in different ways. It was her tween middle daughter that really aggravated her. She pushed back at Jocelyn's suggestions of how she should behave. She was ultra-sensitive when corrected and very particular about how she did things and how she wanted to be spoken to. In Jocelyn's mind, *this kid wants to run the show*. Jocelyn got fed up pretty quickly with her and found herself emotionally flooded daily. When her daughter even looked like she was ready to engage in some kind of pushback, the hair on the back of Jocelyn's neck stood up. She was ready for battle.

That was me with Justin. If that's where you are or are headed with your parenting, we are here to give you hope that it can be turned around with a technique that can take you from triggered to calm.

JUSTIN: I can remember as a child wanting to respond positively to what my parents asked of me, but something happened when I turned 8. I became very curious about the world I lived in and my place in it. At that point in my life, every question I asked adults—or specifically my parents—came from a place of inquiry, not defiance.

After a few disappointing answers and unsatisfactory conclusions, I spent a lot of time alone trying to figure myself out. Many times, this seemed problematic for my parents, as evidenced by their reactions to me. Looking back, I know some of my actions triggered them and made them do and say things that were dismissive and frustrating. My frustration and disappointment later turned to anger and distrust.

These unregulated emotions negatively affected many aspects of my life. I started to care less and act up more in school. Managing my confidence and self-esteem became a daily battle. Making friends was easy but keeping them got a lot harder.

All of this was happening outside the comfort of my own home, so the last thing I needed was any of these things happening in my household, but they were. There was no escape from being challenged for who I am or the conclusions I drew about the world we live in. When I tried to explain my reasoning and actions, my parents would say things like "You're being dramatic" or "You *never* listen." For my parents, the superheroes of my life, their inability to regulate their emotions made me question my safety in bringing difficult conversations to them.

LYNNE: As Justin's mom, what I was experiencing at that time was a child who always seemed resistant to trusting that his parents knew best and were not trying to silence and control him. Phone calls from his school triggered my fears, especially as the mom of a young Black boy, and I would tighten the reins even more.

I know it's easy as a parent to give in to your triggers and just exert your parental power over your child. But the cost to your relationship is high. They may isolate, hide things, turn to their friends over you, or become depressed. That's what was happening with Justin, and I was really scared. Honestly, I was afraid that we were going to lose him. I needed to do something to turn things around. I had to learn to be like water.

Let me continue...

What Does It Mean to Be Like Water?

"Be like water. Adjust to the object, and you will find your way around or through it. If nothing within you stays rigid, outward things will disclose themselves. Be like water, my friend." This, in case you are wondering, is a Bruce Lee quote that feels relevant.

My mind and my parenting started to change once I began developing this technique; unfortunately, Bruce left no instructions for how to actually "Be Like Water." It has been a beneficial practice for managing emotions and letting go of rigid thinking, rules, and cultural norms that get in the way of flowing from an empty vessel. Scary sounding in theory, both challenging and liberating in practice.

Being like water means being able to be still, then rise in a situation, act with strength and consciousness, and return to a place of calm stillness. It clears the way for your best choices.

Getting to this state isn't easy, but for myself and the majority of my clients, practicing it has been calming and even fun. It will challenge your patience. It can be time-consuming, and some people never get there completely, but trying to be like water for even two minutes can lower your stress level in the moment and shift the conversation enough for your child to begin to open up to you.

Allow me to continue...

My First Try

"Be like water, be like water, Lynne, be like water." I needed to repeat this because at the moment, I was much more inclined to be like fire and just burn. Ten-year-old Justin had forgotten his homework and books at school. This was something that he had done at least three times a week since the start of school, and it was December. In spite of countless questions and reminders, we had spent way too many Saturdays pleading with the security guard to let us into the classroom to retrieve all of his materials, and this time, I was ready to blow.

What water was up against was frustration, fatigue, confusion, embarrassment, all ready to explode into anger. Knowing that anger sits atop so many emotions, I knew I had to go deep and identify those emotions to do some serious inquiry. I knew this because before I could make it to water, I did in fact explode, and it was close to volcanic. It turns out it is not easy to be like water, my friend.

In that moment of explosion, I was terrified. It was not the norm for me to explode, and I feared this would not stop the endless "forgetfulness" and "unfocused" way Justin seemed to be going through life.

As I turned inward to inquiry, I tapped into the feelings of confusion—why on earth was this child so forgetful? Frustration—why couldn't he at least remember when we were still at the school? Fatigue—going through this same scene week after week was exhausting. And then, darn it, embarrassment—why is my child the only child that is doing this? What is everyone thinking about him and me, his mom? It was at this point that I felt more like sinking underneath the water rather than being water, and yet I knew I had to try.

JUSTIN: My mom is right—I wasn't a forgetful child. At this point, I had started to realize that no matter how hard I tried, school wasn't for me, and the majority of adults who were responsible for caring about my future didn't care at all about me. After all, none of them tried to find out why I might be forgetting things regularly.

LYNNE: Justin speaks the truth. It is through employing the technique of being like water over the course of several months that I was able to turn my focus to researching why these things might be happening. I found out that he wasn't forgetful, lazy, unfocused, disinterested in school, or defiant. He had a learning difference. A learning difference that goes undiagnosed in thousands of children and adults. Parenting tests every opposition to being like water. Our children and the situations surrounding their lives push every button, fire off old and new triggers, and stretch and stress us to what we believe are our limits. The idea that in today's world we could take the time to learn to be like water and then actually prioritize being like water rather than avoid, yell, order, fix, explode, or let the fear rise up in you and drive you to a substance break is worth much questioning. And yet I know that it can be done.

Again, I'll continue...

The Process of Being Like Water

Step 1: Sit still or stand and simply listen to what is being said. (This can be uncomfortable, but listen through your discomfort.)

Step 2: Observe their facial expressions and any other non-verbals. Body language gives you clues about what they are feeling.

Step 3: Remind yourself to be like water, move gently, swaying like water. (It doesn't have to be big movements. Swaying is a self-regulatory action that reduces stress, lowers blood pressure, and works on the parasympathetic nervous system.)

Step 4: Take note of your own feelings. (Do not worry about what they may think about what you are doing—water knows its power and does not react but rather gives what is needed.)

Step 5: Ask a question and then listen some more while still swaying like water. It is a gentle movement, not a storm.

Step 6: Tune in fully to both your body, including your breathing, and what is happening and being said. (At this time, your goal is to move toward calm and consciousness.)

Step 7: Continue breathing and swaying, staying present with both yourself and your child.

Step 8: Breathe in and out, trying to match your sway. (You are taking in everything that they are saying, even if they are heated.)

Step 9: Pause your swaying and give your best response. Water adapts to the circumstance. Adapt to the reality that this is happening, and you can flow with it.

Step 10: Continue the conversation in this flow—swaying, listening, breathing, responding. (It takes some practice, but you can get there.)

It's not a quick fix, but it is powerful. It helped me open up to a greater understanding of Justin and to some deep conversations we still have to this day.

Dr. Lynne Maureen Hurdle (she/her) is a communication expert and conflict resolution strategist, best-selling author, leadership coach, proud mom, and Bronx girl with over 40 years of experience blending communication, conflict, and culture. She has taught conflict-resolution skills to parents in schools across the world. She co-hosts the television show *Working It Out Across Generations.*

Justin Hurdle-Price (he/him/his) is a speaker, facilitator, and strategic communication specialist who began facilitating conflict-resolution workshops for young people and adults at age 10. He has co-facilitated workshops in schools, for nonprofits, and at national conflict-resolution conferences across the country. He worked as a trainer and coach for youth from all different backgrounds and helped design workshops for tweens, teens, parents, teachers, and young adults. He is the co-host of *Working It Out Across Generations,* a TV show that helps bridge multigenerational perspectives in everyday conflict.

Download Lynne and Justin's free Conflict Resolution Toolkit at www.lynnemaureenhurdle.com.

ANCHORED THROUGH THE STORM: MORNING BATTLES TO MEANINGFUL CONNECTION WITH YOUR NEURODIVERGENT TEEN

Amanda Baker

———

By 7:38 a.m., I had already raised my voice.

The kitchen felt crowded — not just with bodies, but with urgency. One son needed to leave earlier for elementary school. The other had a later high school start but was still half in sleep mode, staring at the fridge like the answer to life might be behind the yogurt. I was at the stove making eggs. Toast popped up. The kettle hissed. My blood pressure rose.

"Mom, I need this signed."

"Signed for what?"

"The field trip. Today. And twenty dollars."

"Today?"

"I told you."

Cabinet doors slammed. My voice shifted from calm to heated. The more I pushed — "Why am I only seeing this now?" — the smaller he got. Shoulders hunched. One-word answers. His brother muttered, "You always wait until the last minute," his words sharp in the air. The clock kept moving. I kept talking. And the gap between us widened in real time.

There it was — that familiar spiral. Not because anyone was "misbehaving," but because three nervous systems were colliding over a last-minute permission slip. Bodies tense, words clipped, presence shrinking. I was carrying my own invisible load of schedules, deadlines, and expectations. Understanding it all didn't stop my frustration.

Moments like that morning made me realize something had to change. For parents of neurodivergent teens, mornings can feel overwhelming — sudden demands, strong emotions, and sensory and executive-functioning challenges collide in ways that escalate stress for both parent and teen. What made the difference for me was creating space to align, connect, and feel empowered — what I now call the ACE Approach. Applying it transformed mornings from high-stress battles into opportunities for connection, growth, and resilience.

The 7:00 A.M. Storm

Theory only becomes meaningful in practice — every sensory trigger, delayed step, and sibling interaction tests patience and presence. To illustrate, let's step into a composite household, drawn from patterns I've observed across over 400 families raising neurodivergent children and teens.

Elena's mornings are a delicate balancing act. Her son Noah [16], on the autism spectrum, gifted, and prone to social anxiety, is still in bed, headphones on, curtains drawn. Each tick of the clock tightens the knot in her stomach. Rushing him will heighten his anxiety, yet every minute counts: Has he remembered his homework? Will he navigate the bathroom without frustration? Will he tolerate breakfast smells and sibling chatter?

Ava [14] debates what to wear, back-and-forth between choices that feel trivial but are time-consuming. Liam [12] is glued to his iPad, oblivious to the clock. Elena moves between the kitchen and hallway, repeating instructions that Noah may hear but not process. Breathing deeply helps, but kitchen noise pushes her nerves higher.

Noah finally emerges from the bedroom for the bathroom. The lights, the household noise — each small step feels monumental. Elena hovers, torn between giving him space and guiding him through tasks before it's time to leave. Every pause, sigh, or muttered word spikes tension. Regulated presence feels nearly impossible as minutes slip away.

By the time Noah exits the bathroom, Ava is frustrated over her clothing, and Liam still stalls over the iPad. Elena sinks into a chair for a brief moment, exhaling, acknowledging the fragility of these mornings — how quickly one small disruption can ripple through the household.

Research comparing parents of neurodivergent and neurotypical children shows that caregivers of autistic and ADHD youth experience markedly higher stress. Studies also indicate that when parents receive support to use positive, problem-focused coping strategies and access social support, family well-being improves and children demonstrate fewer emotional and behavioral difficulties.[10] Understanding these patterns — and why familiar "fix-it" strategies often fall short — is essential. The ACE Approach is designed to provide that kind of structured support, offering parents practical tools to reduce daily tension, strengthen regulation, and guide their neurodivergent teens with greater steadiness.

Navigating the Storm with the ACE Approach

Can mornings really change? The answer is yes — but not instantly. Change doesn't mean your teen will follow every instruction perfectly; it means creating moments where cooperation, understanding, and steadiness are possible, even amid the unpredictability of adolescence.

That's the essence of the ACE Approach: **Aligned, Connected, Empowered**.

Being **aligned** means noticing your own reactions before responding — acting from intention rather than impulse — helping prevent escalation when time pressure or tension spikes.

Connection is tuning in to your teen's experience. A brief acknowledgement, calm question, or pause of empathy can invite engagement, reduce resistance, and reinforce trust without demanding perfection.

Empowerment involves practical scaffolds and predictable routines. Structured choices, visual cues, or breaking tasks into smaller steps can make mornings more manageable. Empowerment supports teen independence while easing conflict and frustration.

Research on co-regulation shows that when caregivers manage their own emotional responses and offer consistent, attuned support, adolescents develop stronger self-regulation over time.[11] In other words, your steadiness becomes the scaffold for your teen's steadiness. ACE works by addressing the "why" behind behavior. Teens often resist or withdraw not to frustrate you, but to cope with emotional overload, transitions, executive-functioning demands, or sensory input. Recognizing the root cause shifts your response from irritation to curiosity, allowing collaboration to replace tension.

Some mornings may show immediate improvement — smoother transitions, less pushing and prodding. Lasting change emerges over weeks and months of consistent practice. Progress often appears quietly: a calmer response, a task completed without prompting, or a teen who handles pressure with more ease.

Putting ACE into Action

Frameworks sound steady and reassuring on paper. Mornings rarely do.

For Elena, change didn't start with a routine chart taped to the fridge. It began with a pause — small enough to miss, powerful enough to shift everything.

It was 7:12 a.m. The clock felt loud. Ava was calling from down the hall. Liam was arguing with his shoelaces. Noah's door was still closed.

Elena's chest tightened. We're running out of time.

Her old script rose quickly: He should be up. He knows the routine.

Alignment meant catching that script before it spilled out. It meant interrupting autopilot. It meant asking herself a harder question: *What kind of parent do I want to be in this moment?*

She walked to Noah's doorway instead of shouting down the hall. The curtains were drawn tight. His headphones hummed faintly. He huddled under the blanket, shoulders tight, bracing for the day ahead.

For a second, she almost pulled the curtains open. Instead, she softened her voice.

"Your body looks tense," she said gently. "Is it hard to get started?"

Silence. Then one headphone slid halfway off.

"It's already too loud," he muttered. "And I can't find my math folder. I'm going to get in trouble."

There it was — not defiance, but anxiety colliding with the ticking clock.

Elena allowed herself to notice that. Her shoulders dropped. Her breath slowed.

"So your brain's already loud," she reflected, "and now you're worried about math."

He nodded, eyes half-closed. Connection is rarely dramatic. It is this — being accurately seen without correction.

Something subtle shifted. The tension didn't disappear, but it loosened, just enough to create movement.

"Okay," she said. "Let's keep it dim for a minute. Do you want two minutes under the blanket, or should I look for the folder while you brush your teeth?"

Choice within structure. Calm within urgency. Empowerment without abandonment.

The morning wasn't seamless. Ava still huffed about clothing. Liam still stalled. Noah still moved slowly. But he moved. Not because he was pushed, but because he felt understood instead of pressured.

That is the heart of ACE. Alignment steadies the parent. Connection regulates the relationship. Empowerment builds competence and cooperation.

Change didn't happen all at once. The first few mornings, Elena questioned herself. Was she too soft? Too controlling? Trust in this new approach, especially after months of tense mornings, didn't appear overnight. Some days were smoother. Others slid backwards.

The real growth began in reflection. Later that week, after the house was quiet, Elena replayed the morning in her mind. Not to criticize, but to notice: Where had she stayed aligned? Where had urgency crept in? What helped Noah move forward? What escalated Ava? What shifted Liam from the screen to the front door?

That evening, she gently checked in with Noah.

"Mornings have felt a little different," she said. "What's helping?"

He shrugged at first. Then: "You don't come in mad anymore."

It wasn't elaborate. But it confirmed what she had sensed. Her tone had been the tipping point more often than the missing math folder.

Reflection isn't just looking at your teen's behavior. It's examining your own patterns — the speed of your voice, the tension in your jaw, the stories you tell yourself about what "should" happen. It's adjusting the environment before adjusting expectations.

Together, changes emerged: packing the math folder after dinner, keeping headphones within reach. Intentional adjustments. Small steps forward.

Even with alignment, connection, and empowerment in place, implementation is rarely smooth. Old habits resurface. Time pressure returns. Teens test limits. Parents second-guess themselves. The storm doesn't vanish simply because you've anchored. The difference is this: with ACE, you no longer face the morning in reactive chaos. You have a structure that helps you notice, respond, and repair. You turn tension into information, guilt into growth, and disruption into opportunity.

When the Storm Pushes Back: Common Challenges in Using ACE

No framework eliminates friction, especially in homes with neurodivergent teens. Mornings often arrive like storms, and a man I'll call Daniel, father of a thirteen-year-old with ADHD, knows this well. His son's mornings once unfolded with scrolling on the phone until the last possible moment, then panicking when things weren't ready. Daniel's instinct was to lecture about responsibility — a pattern that predictably led to slammed doors and silent car rides.

Urgency is one of the first challenges parents face. Buses don't wait, and emotions spike when time is short. Daniel learned that it was hardest when he felt the pressure the most.

Connection can feel risky. Initially, validating his son's frustration seemed permissive. Daniel worried that slowing down would let tasks slide. Over time, he discovered that a simple acknowledgment — "It's hard to switch gears in the morning, huh?" — allowed cooperation to emerge without removing expectations.

Consistency is another hurdle. At first, his son shrugged, rolled his eyes, or ignored the checklist. Daniel worried he was failing. By evening, Daniel's mind was exhausted from work, appointments, and parenting demands, leaving little energy to try out new strategies.

Modification became key. Daniel started small: focus on the first ten minutes of the morning, offer structured choices, and reflect each evening on his own triggers. Gradually, progress appeared — fewer explosions, fewer slammed doors, and a calmer drive to school.

Obstacles are not evidence that ACE isn't working; they are part of the recalibration. The storm may still arrive each morning, but with alignment, connection, and empowerment, you are no longer standing in it without an anchor.

Your ACE Compass

Mornings with a neurodivergent teen can feel unpredictable—rushed, loud, and full of tension. The ACE Approach offers a practical compass to navigate these moments. Start with alignment: choose one priority and respond intentionally, rather than reacting to every small crisis. Next, connect: notice your teen's body, emotions, or brief signals before giving instructions. Even a single reflective statement or gentle pause can reduce resistance and invite cooperation. Then, empower: provide structure through predictable steps, visual anchors, or simple choices—for example, asking, "Shower first or breakfast first?" or helping them pack a backpack in manageable chunks. Finally, reflect: at the end of the morning, notice what worked, what escalated tension, and how your own responses shaped the outcome.

Small actions matter. One calm question, one micro-step completed, one acknowledgment of effort—each builds trust, confidence, and resilience. Even on challenging mornings, consistent practice brings quiet wins: a softer tone, a teen who responds with less resistance, and a household that feels a little steadier. Today, pick one challenge and try a single ACE strategy. Observe, adjust, and celebrate every micro-win.

Amanda Baker is a pediatric occupational therapist and parent coach who blends professional expertise with real-life experience as a mom of three, including teens. For over 25 years, she has supported hundreds of families raising children and adolescents—especially neurodivergent kids—who feel overwhelmed by power struggles and emotional intensity. Through a nervous-system lens, Amanda helps parents look beyond behavior and discover practical ways to build regulation, connection, and confidence at home. She serves on the board of The Diverse Village, a nonprofit supporting neurodivergent families on British Columbia's Gulf Islands.

Download her free Attuned Parent Regulation Toolkit and take the first step toward more connection and confidence at home.

SITTING IN THE YUCK: GETTING COMFORTABLE WITH THE UNCOMFORTABLE

Dr. Marcelle Moore

I wonder how many parents have ever experienced moments when they felt so overwhelmed by their teens' big feelings that they moved into hyper-speed to problem-solve and shut them down. By avoiding the "yuck" and staying at surface level, there are lost opportunities to create safety for the *big stuff* to be heard and thought about.

In 2025, one of my children's teenage friends took his own life, cutting his story prematurely short, leaving his family, my child, and so many others heartbroken at the loss of such a wonderfully caring human being.

I will be forever changed by the pain of knowing this teen will never see another sunrise. He was surrounded by people who loved him, yet for reasons that no one will ever know, he was suffering in silence.

When the loss is through suicide, there are so many unanswered questions, many of which are the agonizing ones of *What if I...?*

The Tragic Cost of Avoiding the "Yuck"

Global research identified suicide as the third leading cause of death for teens aged 15 to 19, with rates rising steeply across mid to late adolescence.[12] Research consistently shows that strong, emotionally safe connections with adults significantly reduce risk.

Heartbreakingly, in my two decades of working with teens as a clinical psychologist, so many have disclosed to me that they have had "dark thoughts" and simply don't want to live anymore, but they are too scared to tell anyone because of their shame and fear of the responses they will get. Terrifying for them and hugely confronting for their loved ones.

A common thread in my conversations with parents is: "We didn't know how to ask if they had thoughts of hurting themselves or wanted to die." For many, they quietly avoided the conversation, concerned that asking might increase the chance they would act on their thoughts. As a result, parents often avoid the "yuck" by not digging deep and asking the hard questions, which can have devastating consequences.

Connect to Protect

Teens feel emotions more intensely than adults, but there are times when parents can feel just as flooded.

I am the mother of three teenagers, and I compare parenting them to navigating a frozen Canadian lake. In those *big feeling moments*, there are times I skirt around the outside, desperately trying to keep my feet connected to the solid ice to avoid the moment where I stand in the wrong place and fall into the "yuck" of the freezing water.

What if I were to tell you that the *most* valuable thing I have learned as a mother and in my work with families is that sitting in the "yuck" is the gateway to truly understanding what matters to them. They need us to pause and listen without comment or judgment. When parents can be genuinely curious with words and body language, trust is built, creating a safe haven for the messy and unpredictable challenges of life to be thought about together.

Get Me Out of Here!

As parents, we are not always taught how to sit with our emotions. We rush our teens out of their feelings, not because we don't love them, but because discomfort feels unsafe. This is not a parenting flaw; it is biology.

Many of us rush past our teens' pain because no one sat in the "yuck" with us. That pattern can be interrupted when parents take time to understand their story and how it could affect their parenting.

Circuit Breaking

When parents tell their teens something is "not a big deal; you need to get over it," or if they cut them off and dive into a teaching moment, they emotionally lose them. The armor goes back on, and the vulnerable part retreats, often yelling, "You never listen! You don't understand me!" Followed by the loud bang of the bedroom door and the throbbing repetitive beat of loud music.

Some behaviors need clear, firm boundaries, and some also need a moment to understand the underlying emotional meaning of the pain.

Sometimes parents respond to the outside feelings, the anger, the defiance, when the inside feelings of pain are the ones that need attending to.

The Power of Moving Through the "Yuck"

Teen disconnection and loneliness have never been higher. Many teens have developed self-limiting beliefs where they associate vulnerability with weakness. These beliefs can prevent them from reaching out for help when they experience intense emotions.

Parents need to be present, listening, and validating their teens' emotions even when they feel overwhelmed by their pain. Teens need parents to prioritize connection over control.

What I have learned from parenting my teens and from the courageous teens I have worked with is that when the "yuck" happens, pausing to listen with purpose and enduring the awkward silences is the micro-connection that creates quiet courage, so you will show up when they need you.

The S.I.T. in the "Yuck" Framework

This is how to create a safe space so the hard things can be thought about, step by step.

S—STAY

When there is a chance for a micro-connection, take it! Build daily connections, not just crisis connections.

A 2–5-minute check-in or a daily shared laugh matters. Think about what you want to do and why. Ask yourself, "If I respond with my first thought, are they likely to lean in or pull away?"

Knowing our own triggers before we dive into action can prevent disconnect.

Stay emotionally present. I remember a moment with my teen when I was sitting on the sofa, and they started to talk. Avoiding eye contact, they were able to express some deep-rooted pain they were wrestling with, which I truly believe only happened because I remained silent until they had finished. It takes immense courage for teens to reach out for help.

I—IDENTIFY and VALIDATE

Truly listen. Let your teen finish the story from beginning to end without interruption.

Create space for your teens to explore their intense feelings. Be curious and perhaps say something like, "It sounds like that must have been really hard for you." Name the feeling without minimizing or trying to fix it. Gentle questioning like "I wonder if you maybe felt..." works better than assumptions.

Empathize while normalizing distress. By remaining curious and not judgmental, you signal that asking for help is safe.

Explicitly look for opportunities outside of conflict moments to state things like, "If you ever struggle, I will not be angry. I will help you find support."

T—TRUST THE PROCESS

Let your teen feel their feelings. Keep in mind any boundaries or lessons you want to share; there will be another moment to address them.

Talk about the tough topics *before* there is a crisis. Saying things like: "If you ever feel overwhelmed or hopeless, you can tell me. I won't freak out." Framing questions as a health issue, not a moral failure, helps teens feel safer to open up. These conversations make the space safe before it is needed.

When parents model this for their teens, a strong message is conveyed: "You are not alone; being vulnerable is courageous and not weak."

Sitting in the "Yuck": The Power of Leaning In

Parenting is one of the most difficult jobs in the world. There is no clear map, and life throws unpredictable curveballs that parents do their best to navigate.

Teens learn emotional resilience from watching adults.

Repairing after conflict is crucial as it models the message that nothing is too big to move through; "I am sorry I snapped. Let's reset." These moments prioritize connection over being right.

Golden Nuggets

Lean into your teens, brave the storms, and know that small check-ins matter.

The teen years are messy and unpredictable. While connection won't erase pain, it does something far more powerful—it interrupts loneliness.

Our teens do not need perfect parents; they need parents who show up, sit in the "yuck," and help them to navigate the messy moments of life. I have often joked with my teens, in a moment of repair, that there are times when I still have my L-plates on. (Learner plates, if you're not familiar with the term.) Mistakes are inevitable.

When parents do react, they repair and take responsibility for their actions, giving teens a clear message that the reaction is about the parent and not them. These moments help teens learn that safe relationships are strong enough to hold mistakes, big feelings, and repair, and that conflict does not mean disconnection. They begin to understand that they are not alone with the hard things, leading to more authentic conversations about what truly matters.

Open dialogue saves lives. When a teen feels seen and that they are never too much, the weight of carrying their pain alone begins to lift. By sitting in the "yuck" with them, we show them the power of togetherness.

Dr. Marcelle Moore is a Child and Adolescent Clinical Psychologist with over two decades of experience supporting parents and teens. She specializes in helping families navigate anxiety, depression, self-harm risk, and the "walking on eggshells" experience many parents describe when connecting with their teens.

Her core message: when teens feel safe and seen, they're more likely to stay engaged and build resilience. Through her "Sitting in the Yuck" framework, Dr. Moore equips parents to respond to big feelings without rescuing, fixing, or escalating. She is also the award-winning author of *Even Lions Get Scared.*

Visit www.drmarcellemoore.com to download a free "S.I.T. in the Yuck" worksheet.

BE THE SAFE PLACE THEY LAND

Anna Neve

———

There are certain parts of life that, as parents, we hope and pray we can shield our children from for as long as possible: rejection, heartbreak, loss, trauma, and abuse, just to name a few. But what happens when life happens, and not only does our world crumble, but theirs does too?

June 29, 2024. The phone call none of us saw coming. Acute Myeloid Leukemia. Out of nowhere, my boys' whole world was thrown into disarray. Their Granddad—the man who had been the closest thing they had to a father their entire lives—was rushed to the hospital with no certainty about the outcome. As a single mum raising two tween boys on my own, with no involvement from their biological dads, I knew that Granddad wasn't just a grandparent. He was their anchor, their key male role model, one of the few steady people in their world aside from me.

Just a short 3.5 weeks later, he was gone.

Shattered. I never imagined this would be part of our story.

This was just the tip of the grief iceberg my boys had been navigating, my eldest in particular. With the loss of his key male role model, my then eleven-year-old's whole world changed in irreversible ways.

What on earth does anyone do under these circumstances, especially as a full-time single mum raising two tween boys? One. Day. At. A. Time.

Grace... and then more grace.

[For privacy, I'll call my boys Mr. 11 and Mr. 10—their ages when this journey began.]

Grief, as our little family has come to know, is so incredibly multi-layered and complex. If you are walking this journey in any way, shape, or form, we see you, and our arms are outstretched, ready to embrace you.

With two boys heading into the teens, I knew that if I didn't create space for their grief to breathe, it would go underground—and come out sideways.

Grief is messy, it's uncomfortable, and, as we very quickly learned, it is something many only have the capacity to hold space for, for a short while. We received flowers followed by meals for a week or two, and then that was it. Our extended family went into their own bubbles as they tried to process, and friends no longer knew how to hold space for them. The once occupied spaces now felt ten times emptier—and suddenly we were all alone.

One of the biggest things I've learned is that Mr. 11 tends to open up at the most "inconvenient times"—specifically, right at bedtime when I am beyond ready to tap out and go to bed myself. However, I encourage you to sit with that concept of "inconvenience" for a moment.

Inconvenient by whose standard?

1. Your child's?

2. Your own?

3. A stereotype, maybe?

For myself, it is probably a combination of 1 and 2. Parenting full-time solo can be a lot at the best of times; throw in the turmoil we find ourselves in, and it's an entirely different ballgame.

Over time, I've learned that what I used to call an inconvenience is the perfect time. Everything else for the day is set aside, Mr. 10 is in bed, the dogs are snoozing, and he has my undivided, albeit exhausted, attention. Learning to hold space in this way, along with creating an environment of transparency for my own experiences—the good, the bad, and the ugly—has resulted in Mr. 11 saying some of the sweetest things. Such as: "Mum, I really appreciate the way you explain things to me. It really inspires me." *Oh my heart!*

Let me encourage you right here that sharing your real-life journey in an age-appropriate way is absolutely worthwhile! It creates a deeper connection as they realize we're not all lectures and boundaries. We're heart and compassion; empathy and depth; wholeheartedly here to help them become the best version of themselves!

Not us.

Not the life we wish we had lived.

Their best selves!

We're figuring it out together—it's a team mentality in our house.

Shortly after Granddad passed away, Mr. 11 was having a particularly difficult time, and initially, I tried to connect via shared experience. "Hey mate, I know this is so hard, my relationship with Granddad was tricky too. I know it's not the same as what you're carrying, but please know I can empathize." BAM, instant reaction. "You don't understand! I've never had a dad, and now the closest thing I had to a dad is gone."

My instinct was to talk it through. Big mistake. He didn't need me talking at him—hearing about my experience at that moment. What he needed was space to feel it. What he needed was to just be held.

I've been incredibly blessed with both my boys, and even now, heading into the hormones as Mr. 11 turns 13, we have an incredibly close and honest relationship. A foundation, I believe, formed through my ability to get on their level from a very young age and own my mistakes with them. I yell? Say something slightly too blunt? You name it, whether it takes five minutes, an hour, or a day, I can guarantee you I will be down on their level apologizing. Why, you might ask? So that they understand that even adults make mistakes, and that just because I'm an adult doesn't give me the freedom to be harsh, rude, or disrespectful to them either.

For our boys, a loss of this magnitude may find them grappling for a "band-aid fix." In Mr. 11's case, he asked more questions about his real dad. All met with honesty, even the hardest parts.

Again, the importance of honesty and transparency, even in the most traumatic things for you to relive or acknowledge, is invaluable in your relationship with your son!

I share this story with Mr. 11's permission, as he shared with me that how I've helped him navigate his grief journey in all its layers is worth helping someone else through theirs.

The door was left open for his biological dad 13 years ago, and we've had no effort or contact since. I reached out, and the response was, "I'll do whatever Mr. 11 wants now." I've gently shared with Mr. 11 that he deserves someone who chooses him, who fights for him, and who is willing to be the adult and put in the effort to restore the relationship. It's never a child's responsibility to fix an adult's mistake. Ever. And so, we're continuing to navigate Mr. 11's life on our own.

Early on, both boys had moments where they shut down on me. When we got to the bottom of it, they shared they were worried they'd upset me by talking about Granddad, or that I'd cry when we discussed it. That was hard to hear. They have one childhood, and I never want them to carry my emotional weight.

And so this opened up the perfect conversation for me to share that I may cry, it may be hard at times; however, I always want them to talk. I always want them to come to me with their hard, their messy, their painful, as well as all of the good and incredible moments. In doing so, this led to more beautiful comments from Mr. 11: "Thanks for always having my back, Mum, I've always got yours for things I can help with."

As Mr. 11 and I continued to explore the grief surrounding his granddad, his dad, and his complicated relationship with his uncles, he discovered that he was trying to find a quick fix for the unbearable pain he was facing. So, we began to focus our attention here, at the root cause. Each time the emotions begin to overflow, we simply sit or play, whatever he feels he needs most, and we reflect on his granddad.

We share stories, we discuss his favorite things, and we find ways to bring those elements into the now.

Both the boys are now also working through how they can develop their own meaningful goodbye "ceremony" for their granddad. I realized, as I deep-dived through countless books on grief over this last year, that I assumed the boys had effectively said goodbye at the funeral. But really, that was just another traumatic day in the aftermath of what we never saw coming. Now, when the time is right, we will do something they have planned that honors their unique connection with him.

If you find yourself walking through any version of grief with your child, please know you are not alone. Don't give up on your boy.

Here's what this journey has taught me so far: Connection before correction.

- Ask: "Do you want my opinion or help here, or do you just need to vent?"
- Ask before sharing your own experience—don't lead with it.
- Look for the root cause. The thing they're reacting to is rarely the real issue.
- Make tears welcome.
- No emotion is too big.

If you need help through this journey, please connect. It would be my honor to hold the light and space for you. Don't let yourself sink completely like I did before reaching your hand out to be held. It is just as important that you have support during this time as your child does as well.

And finally, some scripture I found helpful during this season. Perhaps it will comfort you too:

Psalm 34:18: "The Lord is close to the brokenhearted and saves those who are crushed in spirit."

Psalm 147:3: "He heals the brokenhearted and binds up their wounds."

Anna Neve is a Parent Empowerment Coach and international bestselling author, certified by the Jai Institute of Parent Coaching and trained as an NLP Master Practitioner. Through her practice, Chosen Warrior, Anna helps parents heal from past trauma so they can create nurturing environments for their children. She believes that when we heal ourselves first, we become the parents our families need—creating a positive ripple effect that shapes generations to come.

WHAT MY OWN ADVERSITY IN ADOLESCENCE TAUGHT ME ABOUT RAISING TEENS

Meagan Colvin

I did well in school, played sports, volunteered, and held leadership roles. From the outside, everything looked fine. But underneath that image, I was navigating far more than I ever shared with my parents—dating violence, emotional manipulation, confusion about love and responsibility, and later, sexual violence. I carried most of it quietly, confiding in my twin sister far more than in my parents. Looking back now, as a parent myself, I understand something I couldn't see then: when teens face things alone—when they don't feel safe enough to come to us—the distance in the parent-child relationship quietly widens. Moment by moment, silence by silence.

One of the most important roles we play as parents is not just being physically present, but emotionally available—attuned to our teens' inner world, their struggles, their contradictions, and their growing need for autonomy alongside connection and guidance. Over the years, practices like mindfulness, compassion, and self-compassion have transformed not only my mental health and physical health, but the way I parent. They have also allowed me, later in life, to reconnect with my own mother in new ways—reflecting together on what we didn't have language for then, and how the absence of these tools shaped our health and relationship.

As a child and teen, I don't remember feeling particularly close to my parents emotionally. In fact, large parts of my early and middle childhood feel blurry. What I remember more clearly is my rebellious adolescence—the secrets, the adrenaline-filled risks, the parts of my life I carefully hid. I excelled academically and remained involved in sports, volunteering, and leadership, which kept anyone from looking too closely.

The Moments That Shaped My Silence

One memory still stands out. I was grounded for what felt like forever—for riding with my boyfriend, a teen driver, without asking permission first, to buy a bouquet of flowers for a friend's birthday as a surprise gift. To my parents, it was about safety and rules. To me, it felt disproportionate, shaming, and disconnecting. At the time, I didn't have the words for it, but I felt misunderstood.

Now, as a parent, I can see how moments like that can quietly teach teens something unintended: *Love is conditional. Don't tell. Handle it yourself.*

That may have been around the time the sneaking out started. My twin sister and I lived in the countryside, so sneaking out at night was a big deal. One night, we were caught, and in a moment of panic, I told my parents we had left because I was overwhelmed—because my boyfriend had recently told me he was clinically depressed.

That part was true. He had shared this with me weeks earlier in a way that felt alarming and heavy, and I didn't know what to do with it. I was emotionally unequipped. I questioned whether our relationship was somehow responsible for his pain.

About a year later, after we had broken up, he attempted suicide and then used that crisis to pull me back into the relationship. Months later, the relationship ended for good.

I remember feeling numb—emotionally flat. I knew I *should* feel angry, sad, or devastated, but my body had other plans. I now understand that, as dissociation—my nervous system's way of protecting me from emotions it couldn't safely process. At the time, I just felt relief.

What My Body Held

A few years later, in college, I experienced two instances of date rape, almost a year apart. In both cases, alcohol was involved. I had clearly said "NO" when sober, and the actual memory of the event itself and how I got there was absent, but the signs were present the next day.

The first time, I eventually told my parents over the phone. My father responded with something like, "Maybe you shouldn't have drunk so much." I remember the sharp sting of that moment—not just the words, but what they implied. The subtle shift from support to blame.

When parents judge, criticize, minimize, or question their child's experience of abuse, even unintentionally, it deepens the wound. It teaches the child that their pain is inconvenient, shameful, suspect, or their fault. While we cannot always protect our children from harm, we can—and must—believe them, support them, and stand firmly on their side if and when harm comes.

The second time it happened, I don't recall telling anyone for a long time. I woke up bruised and in pain and had to catch a flight to Chile that same day for a study-abroad program. I pushed the experience aside, buried it under logistics and novel experiences, and kept moving, as if nothing had happened. There was no space to process it or get justice, so my body held it instead.

Two years later, I was diagnosed with a chronic autoimmune disease, one that doctors linked to prolonged stress. Years later, through my work studying nervous system science and the long-term impact of adverse childhood experiences on health and well-being, I began to connect the dots. I could see how years of emotional overwhelm, unprocessed trauma, and nervous system dysregulation had been living in my body all along.

That realization was a wake-up call—not just professionally, but personally and as a mother. It deepened my conviction that adolescence is not a phase we simply "get through," but a critical window where support, guidance, and emotional skills can become a lifeline.

From Survival to Support: The CALMS Approach for Parents of Teens

When I look back on my own adolescence, I see a family doing the best it could with the language, tools, and understanding available at the time. Many of the things I carried quietly weren't hidden because of a lack of love, but because we didn't yet have ways of talking about emotional pain, mental health, or trauma.

Teens don't stay silent because parents don't care. Often, they stay silent because they don't yet know how to make sense of what they're experiencing. Support isn't always absent—it's sometimes outpaced by the complexity of what teens are holding. That realization shaped how I think about parenting today—not from a place of regret, but from a place of growth.

What helps teens most in difficult moments is not perfect responses, but presence—parents who are willing to be emotionally available, curious, and grounded, even when the path forward isn't clear.

From that understanding, my signature framework emerged.

The CALMS Approach

Here are the elements of the acronym:

Compassion creates safety. When teens feel met with understanding rather than judgment or minimization, their nervous systems settle, and communication opens. This is co-regulation in action—your calm presence helping their nervous system settle.

Attachment provides a secure base. Secure attachment refers to an ongoing sense of emotional safety in a relationship—knowing there is a trusted parent who is emotionally available, attuned, responsive, and reliable. This secure base allows teens to explore independence while still feeling supported when they need to return.

Limits and Boundaries offer protection and clarity, helping teens build autonomy and self-trust. This means setting clear, predictable limits around safety and explaining the "why" behind them, inviting dialogue rather than imposing rules, teaching that consent is ongoing and can be withdrawn at any time, and helping teens practice saying "no" and noticing discomfort in their bodies.

Mindfulness supports awareness—helping teens notice emotions and body signals without becoming overwhelmed. Simple practices like grounding exercises, mindful breathing, or paying full attention during everyday moments—a walk, a meal, a shower—can help teens develop this awareness.

Self-Compassion is the ability to respond to one's own pain, mistakes, or struggles with kindness rather than harsh self-judgment. It fosters healing and the emotional safety needed for accountability, learning, and growth. As parents, we can model self-compassion by naming our own mistakes with kindness: "I yelled earlier today. I'm human, and I'm working on it." We can normalize struggle by reminding teens that difficulty is part of being human, not a personal failure. And we can respond to teen mistakes with curiosity—focusing on what can be learned rather than assigning blame.

CALMS works because it aligns with how humans grow and heal—through connection, integration, reflection, and practice over time.

Growth is Generational

We are shaped by the families we come from, our environment, the knowledge available to us, and the cultural norms of our time. What matters most is not what we didn't know then, but what we are willing to learn now.

Research increasingly shows that our brains and nervous systems remain capable of change across the lifespan. With the right conditions—safety, connection, and support—we can continue to grow, even after hardship. A secure relationship with a caring parent or adult, alongside practices like mindfulness, adequate sleep, and regular movement, can become powerful protective factors. Growth doesn't erase trauma, and trauma doesn't guarantee growth. But what happens next—and who is present—makes a profound difference.

Presence is powerful, even when it's imperfect. Even small amounts of attunement, repair, and curiosity accumulate. They strengthen relationships and make space for healing—sometimes in our children, and sometimes across generations.

If you want to begin today, start gently. Choose one CALMS pillar and practice it with intention this week. Notice what shifts over the next few weeks, not just in your teen, but in you.

Growth doesn't require perfection. In fact, we often grow and learn the most when we face adversity or make mistakes and reflect on them. The willingness and courage to keep learning together help us grow as parents and as a family.

Meagan Colvin is an adopted, identical twin and a mom of two. She is a parent coach and mindfulness instructor with an MSW and training in applied neuroscience. For parents seeking practical tools, check out her books *Planting Seeds of Well-Being: Self-Care and Emotional Regulation for Kids and Teens* and *Armadillo Armor: Addressing Bullying with Mindfulness and Nonviolent Communication*, available in Spanish and English. Her Mindful Parenting program supports parents in cultivating presence, regulating their nervous systems, practicing self-compassion, and connecting in everyday life.

SECTION FOUR

DEALING WITH SEX, DRUGS & RUNAWAY DIGITAL

———

SEX TALKS: THE KEY TO RAISING WHOLE, HEALTHY, AND HAPPY HUMANS

Amy Lang, M.A.

If you feel anxious, unsure, or tempted to avoid conversations about sex, consent, and relationships with your teen, you are not alone.

At all.

This was me! I was a long-time sexuality educator who'd had hundreds of difficult conversations—and I assumed I'd be a rock star when it came time to educate my own kids.

Then I freaked out when my kid started talking about his penis. Innocent as can be—but my near-panic-attack was a major surprise.

Just like most parents, I really wanted to get this right. Many of us were raised with silence, shame, or flat-out misinformation—and now we're expected to magically do better?

You've heard:

- Wait until they ask.

- Talking about it encourages them to have sex.

- If they are uncomfortable, they are not ready.

- Neurodivergent kids don't really want or need this information.

All of that sounds reasonable. None of it actually works. These ideas also give parents and caregivers an easy way to avoid the conversations altogether. This is especially true when it comes to teens, and even more so for neurodivergent teens. Many parents skip this part of parenting because they assume their teen is not interested, not ready, or knows enough from sex ed at school.

Sexuality is a natural, normal, and healthy part of being human, and everyone has a relationship with it. For teens, bodies change, attraction intensifies, and relationships quickly become more complex. Decisions about sex, boundaries, and intimacy are already on the table for many teens, whether or not you are ready to accept this.

The good news is that this is entirely possible. When you understand how to communicate clearly and effectively, you can feel ready, capable, confident, and even excited about this important part of parenting teens.

Preparation Is the Protection

Most sex education is built around prevention. Do not have sex. Wait. And if you do, use birth control, use condoms, and do not coerce anyone. There is a strong focus on avoiding pregnancy and STIs, and far less attention on how to make healthy decisions or navigate real relationships.

Prevention matters. It is always part of sex education, and without it, sex education does not work. But *preparation* works better, especially for teens who are actively navigating curiosity, pressure, attraction, and social dynamics.

Preparation means getting your teen ready before they're in the moment. Not just what to avoid. How to think. How to communicate. How to decide what's right when things get emotional, awkward, or intense. When sex is on the table, they'll be as ready as they can be. That's the goal.

When I look back at the decisions I made, I wish I'd had an adult who was willing to be open and direct with me about how to make healthy decisions, relationships, consent, and that sex should feel good to me. That someone thought to prepare me for this big part of life.

Think about your own teen years. What if someone had taken the time to *prepare* you for sex and relationships? Would you have made different choices? Felt more confident or less confused? Be a different person?

Most people answer yes, and that makes sense. You didn't get what you needed, and now you are expected to give your teens something you never received.

For autistic, ADHD, and other neurodivergent teens, preparation matters even more. Many need clearer, more direct information, explicit expectations, and repetition. Subtle hints and vague warnings are often ineffective. Clear and concrete communication is what works.

Sex Is About Pleasure, Trust, Consent, and Connection

You may be afraid to communicate with your kid about pleasure—me too. However, this is the main reason people do sexual things, and even though it feels uncomfortable, your teen has a right to know that sex should feel good to both partners. They also need to know it's about connection, trust, communication, and vulnerability—areas where teens are still learning and practicing.

Talking about pleasure does not encourage teens to have sex. It helps them understand that bodies are capable of feeling good and that pleasure is not shameful. It also means making consent clear, concrete, and doable in real situations that they may actually face.

Teens also need to know that people experience gender and sexual orientation in different ways, and that who they are—or who they are attracted to—should be respected, not judged. The suicide rate for LGBTQ+ teens is four times higher than that of the general population. For queer neurodivergent kids, the rate is even higher.

The one thing that keeps LGBTQ+ kids on par with the general population is parental support, even if this feels confusing for you or goes against your values; your teen's mental health matters more than your discomfort.

Pornography and Teens: What Parents Need to Know (and Say)

The average age of first porn exposure is around twelve. I know. It's shockingly young.

Every child will see porn before they graduate from high school. For most kids, that first exposure is accidental. It's a search that takes a wrong turn, a pop-up, something on a friend's phone, or a link in a DM or group chat.

Please don't tell yourself, "Not my kid." If they're online, it's happening. And the better prepared they are, the better off they'll be.

When your teen understands that sex should be wanted, mutual, and respectful, it pushes back on what they're picking up from porn, peers, social media, and AI.

Porn is already shaping how your teen thinks about sex. If you're not helping them sort out what's real, what's fantasy, and what aligns with your values, the internet will fill in the gaps.

The antidote? You.

You can safely assume your teen has seen porn — or will soon. Here are some ideas for starting the conversations:

The very first thing you should tell them is:

"You won't be in trouble if you tell me you've seen porn. I want to make sure you're okay and help you sort through anything that felt confusing, weird, or intense."

Then you can follow up with:

- "Have you ever run into anything sexual online?"

- "What was that like for you?"

- "How did it make you feel?"

- "What do kids at school say about it?"
- "What do you think about it?"

You want your teen to be prepared before they're exposed to porn and to understand that what they're seeing is fantasy, not real life. You also want them to feel safe telling you about it and to get accurate, values-based information from you — not the internet.

If you are their primary sex-ed source, porn loses its power.

You Have More Influence Than You Think

In places with the best teen sexual health outcomes (hello, Netherlands), adults start early and keep communicating. Sexuality is treated as a normal part of life, not a taboo topic that suddenly appears in adolescence.

If you think you are too late to talk with them, I promise you are not. Yes, their peers, porn, and social media are powerful, and maybe they don't want to listen to you, but don't let this hold you back.

You remain the most influential source of values and information about sexuality and relationships.

There is a simple fix for being behind: apologize for not talking with them sooner and tell them it's time. You can also acknowledge that you might act weird and uncomfortable because no one did this for you, and you don't know what you're doing.

Influence does not come from one big talk. It comes from being steady, calm, and available over time. From initiating conversations. From answering questions honestly. From having 2000 two-minute conversations. From not making it weird.

One of my proudest parenting moments is when my son told me he was planning to have sex and wanted to make sure I knew he was being safe on all fronts. *He was prepared.* He trusted me enough to tell me. I was thrilled.

Trust is one of the most protective factors for teens. When your teen knows they will not be shut down, punished, or shamed, they are far more likely to ask real questions, confide in you, seek help early, and make decisions that align with your family values.

What Kids Need to Know, and When

This is a very general guide to help you get ahead of what kids will learn from unsafe or inaccurate sources. For neurodivergent kids, timing may shift. Some will need information earlier, some later, and many will need repetition. Development, not age alone, should guide these conversations.

Sharing this information teaches your kids that you are their most trustworthy source when it comes to sex and relationships.

Middle School

Middle school is a critical bridge between childhood and adolescence. Bodies are changing quickly, social pressure increases, and curiosity often spikes. It's also the time when conversations about gender and orientation, romantic relationships, porn, and sex amp up. This can be confusing, especially for neurodivergent kids.

To get ahead of this—and loads of misinformation—by the time they start middle school, *they should know the basics of everything.*

By the end of middle school, kids should know:

- What consent looks like in real situations, including pressure, coercion, and manipulation.

- That sex should be wanted, mutual, and respectful.

- It is always okay to say no, change your mind, or set boundaries at any point.

- How emotions, attraction, and hormones can influence decision-making.

- What people mean when they talk about sex and common sexual behaviors.

- The basics of contraception and STI prevention.

Middle schoolers need help separating reality from misinformation, and when you stay engaged and push through your discomfort during this stage, it provides a crucial reality check.

High School

Worried about giving your high schooler too much information? Don't. "Too much information" should be your goal—you can talk with them about everything.

One caveat: neurodivergent teens may need slower pacing or more selectivity—some are prone to blurting or are developmentally behind peers.

Throughout high school, the focus should deepen:

- Healthy and unhealthy relationship patterns, including respect, power, and control.

- Communicating boundaries, making decisions, and responding to pressure.

- How and where to access birth control, medical care, testing, and support.

- Pleasure, responsibility, and readiness.

- Detailed contraception and STI information.

- Understanding consent as ongoing, mutual, and revocable at any point.

How to Start Without Making It a Big Deal and Top 10 Sex Talk Tips

You just need to start.

Here are some of my best tips for communicating with teens:

- Keep it short. Two or three minutes is enough. No one likes a lecture.

- Talk side by side while doing something else—driving, walking, or doing dishes. Distraction helps, especially with neurodivergent kids.

- Ask, "What do you think?" and pause long enough to hear the answer.

- Use the world around you. Shows, podcasts, social media, and overheard comments can all be easy entry points.

- Ask what other kids are saying. Teens often talk more about peers than themselves.
- Say when you feel awkward and keep going. You are modeling how to handle hard conversations.
- Be clear about what porn is, how it influences people, and why it is not real sex or real relationships.
- Share the load with another parent or trusted adult.

Use every tool you have: books, teen-friendly videos, texts, notes, everyday moments, and your own voice.

Final Thoughts

Talking with teens about sex, consent, and relationships requires presence, honesty, and a willingness to keep showing up. When you provide accurate information and clear values, teens are better equipped to make healthy decisions. That's how you raise a whole, healthy, happy human.

So, put on your big-kid pants and go for it. You do not need to get this perfectly right to make a real difference. Showing up and making an effort matter more than having all the answers.

No one will die, and no one will throw up. Promise.

Amy Lang, M.A., is a sexuality and parent educator and a sexual abuse prevention specialist. She's helped thousands of parents around the world have the birds-and-bees talks with more confidence and ease. She also holds a certification in neurodiversity and sexuality and helps parents of neurodivergent kids—and the professionals who support them—communicate openly about sexuality and relationships. She is the author of *Sex Talks With Tweens: What to Say & How to Say It*. Grab a copy of this script-based book so you don't have to figure out what to say because Amy's done it for you.

HELP! MY TEEN HAS BECOME SEXUALLY ACTIVE! WHAT NOW?

Rebecca Reber

———

You accidentally saw a text, overheard a conversation, or, in a heated argument, your teen told you they had become sexually active. Your heart races, your blood pressure spikes, you want to cry and scream, and the urge to vomit is overwhelming. You may want to lock your teen in their room until they graduate from college. Let me assure you, these reactions are completely normal. Learning that your teen has become sexually active requires some serious, tough conversations. As parents, we must lead these conversations with a calm head, listening ears, and genuine love.

When puberty hits and hormones rage, parents need to prepare themselves for the possibility that their teen will become sexually active. According to the CDC, 32% of high school students report having had sexual intercourse.[17] The 2023-2024 CDC's National Survey of Family Growth says that between the ages of 15 and 19, almost 50% of teens have engaged in oral sex. Parents must have a plan for guiding their teens through this, preferably having had an open dialogue about sex ed and healthy relationships throughout their child's life. These lifelong conversations may delay your teen from becoming sexually active in high school because they have already learned about the responsibilities and consequences of sexual behavior. We must always listen, give medically accurate information, and share our family's beliefs and morals about sex in a loving way. We want to lay a foundation where our teens feel safe asking questions or discussing relationships with us. Using shame, anger, or punitive measures regarding sex will create a barrier between you and your child, and it is very unlikely they will ever feel safe coming to you for help or advice. Parents of LGBTQ+ teens may find that their conversations look a little different, but they should always be grounded in love, affirmation, and acceptance. All parents should be prepared to discuss same-sex experiences with their teens in a nonjudgmental, inclusive, and supportive manner.

Why This Conversation Matters

I spent 24 years of my teaching career working with pregnant and parenting teens in a high school setting. Most of these young parents received little to no sex education from their parents and guardians prior to becoming pregnant. When they became sexually active and eventually ended up pregnant, I saw many instances where parents handled the news poorly, and it had devastating effects on the teen and the family. Teen mothers found themselves homeless or moving into boyfriends' homes. I saw instances of domestic violence, substance abuse, sex trafficking, illnesses due to STIs, and repeat pregnancies while living with the boyfriend's family. Teen mothers dropped out of high school. This lack of education kept them reliant on their boyfriends and their boyfriends' families—they were stuck in bad situations with very limited futures. I saw family relationships broken forever. I believe that if the parents had handled the conversation differently, these young parents would have had far more positive life outcomes.

One former teen parent told me, "I was 16 years old, pregnant, and my parents kicked me out. I was living in an apartment with my son's father, and there was no stability. Our electricity was shut off at times. I was trying to finish school while he worked a minimum-wage job at 45-50 hours a week. We were constantly arguing out of frustration with our situation. No money, no car, and I was financially dependent on him."

My daughter recently came to me because a close friend of hers had become sexually active. I spent the beginning of the conversation just listening, then I began to gently talk about the responsibilities and consequences her friend might face by engaging in sex. My daughter asked questions, and I answered honestly. Using her friend's story, I was able to educate my daughter about important aspects of sexual health before she ever became sexually active.

So, what do parents do when they find out their teen has become sexually active? We must take some deep breaths and center our emotions. When we feel that we have achieved this, we must go into educator mode. We need our teens to understand that becoming sexually active is serious, includes risks, and could potentially change their lives.

What to Talk About

Here's what I've learned matters most in these conversations—not as a checklist to get through, but as areas to explore together, following your teen's lead:

1. Is your teen *physically* okay after the sexual experience?

   Was it consensual? Were they pressured into it? If your teen was raped, then a doctor's exam and police report need to be filed immediately. Depending on the situation of the sexual encounter, counseling may be helpful for your teen.

2. Is your teen *emotionally* okay after the sexual experience?

   Are they in a relationship? Or was it a random hook-up? Is there still contact with the other person involved, and is that contact positive or negative? Help your teen understand that people can have very different expectations about what sex means. One person might be looking for an emotional connection while the other is more casual. Talking through these differences will help them understand sexual relationships for the rest of their lives.

3. *Why* did your teen become sexually active?

   Were they pressured or coerced? Were they afraid of losing a boyfriend/girlfriend because they wouldn't engage in sexual behaviors? Were they looking for attention or validation?

These questions are great lead-ins for discussing healthy relationships.

4. Did they use birth control and STI *protection* during the sexual encounter?

    Do they know the consequences of intercourse and oral sex? Could they have contracted an STI? For our daughters, have they missed any periods? This is a parent's opportunity to teach about safe sex.

5. If your teen plans to continue being sexually active, do they have a birth control and STI *prevention plan?* Do they have a *pregnancy plan?*

    Parents may need to help their teen create these.

6. Schedule a *doctor's appointment.*

    Both genders should be tested for STIs, and if they continue being sexually active, they should be tested every year. If at any time they start showing symptoms of an STI, they should be tested. Females should be monitored for a missed period, and a pregnancy test should be administered.

When You Get It Wrong

What happens if you completely fall apart, yell, and scream when finding out that your teen has become sexually active? Good parents get overwhelmed, flustered, and angry at times. We all make mistakes as parents. My best advice is to approach your teen with full transparency—let them know that you were wrong in how you reacted. Let them know you shouldn't have blown up at them, and you are truly sorry. They may be wary at first and resist talking to you—but don't give up!

1. Ask for a do-over, a chance to sit down and talk with them. You may have to ask a couple of times before they are ready to talk.

2. When they are ready, your job is to just listen.

3. Hug them. Tell them you love them no matter what, and nothing will ever change that.

4. Tell them that you have questions and concerns, and then gently begin the conversation as outlined above. The conversations should not happen all in one day or in one sitting. This should be an ongoing conversation, and your teen should understand that it's serious because it is.

The Conversation Doesn't End There

If your teen is sexually active, it is important that they understand you will remain involved in this area of their life. Conversations about sexual health and relationships should be ongoing, not one-time discussions. Sexual activity carries emotional, physical, and relational complexities, and your continued guidance reflects care and responsibility, not control. While teens often desire the independence of adulthood, they are still minors navigating adult decisions. Establishing clear expectations that you will check in regularly helps reinforce accountability, safety, and open communication.

Discovering that your teen is sexually active can be challenging for many parents. Adolescents often experience embarrassment, fear, or anxiety when they realize their parents are aware, particularly if they are uncertain about how their parents will respond. Responding with calmness, empathy, and a nonjudgmental approach creates space for honest dialogue and ongoing communication. When teens feel safe rather than shamed, they are more likely to seek guidance and make informed decisions. The education and values we communicate about relationships and sexual health during adolescence can significantly influence long-term well-being, shaping both their health and future relationships.

Rebecca Reber is an internationally best-selling author, early childhood teacher, and educational speaker who has led a Teen-Parent program in Southern California for over two decades. She earned her Bachelor of Science in Child Development from Cal Poly, San Luis Obispo. Rebecca's mission is to help parents build the confidence to talk with their children about tough topics—from healthy relationships to sex ed—starting early and in developmentally appropriate ways. Her passion is giving families the tools, language, and courage to help kids grow up informed, safe, and supported. She is a mom to a young adult son and teenage daughter.

Visit Rebecca's website to receive free topic prompts for parents of sexually active teens.

THE SILENT EPIDEMIC: TEEN MARIJUANA DEPENDENCY

Susan Notis

———

"Am I Overreacting?" Many parents come to this concern quietly. They notice changes—motivation slipping, emotional volatility increasing, school engagement fading, a once-connected teen pulling away. An internal sense of alarm begins to grow, even as they try to reassure themselves it's "just a phase." And when they voice that concern, they are often met with messages from other parents or the broader culture that minimize what they're seeing.

"It's just weed."

"It's safer than alcohol."

"Everyone experiments."

"You're overreacting."

These responses are common, especially in a time when marijuana use is increasingly normalized and legally accepted. But for the parents I work with, living with the day-to-day reality, that messaging doesn't always match their experience, often leaving them feeling confused, angry, and deeply isolated.

This chapter is not written to provoke panic. It's written because we are underestimating a real and growing public health issue: teen marijuana dependency in a culture that often treats cannabis as harmless.

Why Today's Marijuana Poses Real Risks for Teens

Many parents instinctively compare what they're seeing now to what they remember from their own adolescence. That comparison is understandable, but it no longer reflects the reality teens are navigating today.

Marijuana today is far more potent than it was decades ago. Studies tracking cannabis in the United States show that THC levels, the compound responsible for marijuana's psychoactive effects, have increased over time. What once averaged around 2–4% THC in the 1970s and 1980s has risen to 15–25% THC in many commonly available products today, with some products containing even higher concentrations.[18]

Higher THC levels increase the intensity of marijuana's effects, accelerate tolerance, and raise the risk of dependency, especially for developing brains.

Form and Access Matter

How marijuana is used has also changed. It is now available in many forms, making dosing unpredictable and effects harder to anticipate. For teens, who cannot legally purchase marijuana, vape cartridges sold by dealers are increasingly being found laced with other substances, introducing risks beyond marijuana itself.

Together, higher potency and unpredictable dosing make it easier for use to escalate quietly, without clear or immediate warning signs.

Why Teens Are Especially Vulnerable

Adolescence is not just a social or emotional transition; it is a period of significant brain development. The teenage brain is still under construction, particularly in areas responsible for judgment, impulse control, emotional regulation, and long-term planning.

Adults tend to rely more heavily on the prefrontal cortex, the part of the brain involved in reasoning, foresight, and weighing consequences. In teens, this system is still developing. As a result, decision-making, especially under stress or strong emotion, is more likely to be guided by the brain's emotional centers, such as the amygdala. So, when emotions run high, their brains are still learning how to pause, regulate, and consider long-term outcomes.

Reward, Relief, and the Developing Brain

During adolescence, the brain's reward and motivation systems are especially responsive. Dopamine pathways, responsible for learning what feels good, what relieves discomfort, and what to repeat, are highly active during the teen years.

Substances like marijuana can temporarily alter these systems, creating feelings of calm, pleasure, or escape. For a teen navigating stress, anxiety, neurodiversity, or emotional pain, that relief can feel powerful and immediate.[19]

Because the connections between emotional processing, reward, and decision-making are still maturing, teens often struggle to pause, weigh consequences, or accurately assess risk in the moment. This can make repeated use more likely and accelerate the path from experimentation to dependency.

When Use Turns Into Dependency

Despite common belief, research now clearly shows that cannabis can be addictive. Cannabis Use Disorder is a recognized medical diagnosis, and studies estimate that about 1 in 6 adolescents who use marijuana will develop dependency.[20]

Cannabis dependency doesn't always look dramatic at first. But, over time, teens may start to present with symptoms that parents do not initially connect to marijuana use.

A recent CDC analysis found that cannabis-related emergency visits among youth have increased significantly. The steepest rise occurred among girls ages 11–14, while teens and young adults ages 15–24 now account for over 90% of cannabis-related emergency visits among those under 25.[21]

One increasingly recognized condition is Cannabis Hyperemesis Syndrome (CHS), a pattern of severe, repeated vomiting associated with long-term, frequent cannabis use. Episodes can include intense nausea, dehydration, abdominal pain, and vomiting. In clinical settings, this extreme presentation is sometimes referred to colloquially as "scromiting," a term parents may identify with because the distress of vomiting and screaming at the same time can be intense and frightening.

What makes CHS especially challenging is that marijuana is often believed to relieve nausea, leading teens to use more in an attempt to stop symptoms, unintentionally worsening the cycle.

Beyond CHS, prolonged heavy use has also been linked to increased emotional volatility, anxiety, paranoia, sleep disruption, and, in some, psychotic episodes.

It's also important to understand that frequent marijuana use can mask or mimic underlying mental health and neurodevelopmental challenges. Symptoms of anxiety, depression, attention difficulties, or mood disorders are often difficult to assess accurately while cannabis is in someone's system, which can delay clear diagnosis and appropriate support.

In addition to physical and emotional changes, regular cannabis use during adolescence has been linked to declines in academic performance and school attendance, as well as higher rates of school dropout.[22]

This deserves to be said clearly: None of this means a teen is "broken," and it does not mean parents have failed. I see marijuana dependency in many well-intentioned, educated, and caring families. Dependency reflects the interaction between a developing brain, a powerful substance, and a culture that promotes cannabis use—not a lack of character or care.

What Actually Helps Change Take Root

When parents begin to recognize that marijuana use has turned towards dependency, the instinct is often to push harder with more warnings, more lectures, more pressure to stop.

That response is understandable. It comes from fear, love, and a desire to protect.

But research in addiction and adolescent development points to a difficult truth: lasting change is most likely when motivation comes from within. Change that is forced or coerced may interrupt behavior in the short term, but it rarely creates durable progress on its own.

This does not mean parents should do nothing. And it does not mean boundaries disappear.

It means that *how* parents communicate, respond, and set limits matters as much as *what* they say. Approaches that increase defensiveness or power struggles often strengthen resistance, while approaches that reduce conflict and reinforce healthy behavior can quietly support a teen's readiness for change over time.

Evidence-based family approaches, including Community Reinforcement and Family Training (CRAFT), have consistently shown that reducing resistance, reinforcing healthy behavior, and holding clear boundaries can increase the likelihood of change over time. My work is informed by these principles.[23]

Equally important, these models emphasize something parents often neglect: their own regulation and well-being. Parents who remain grounded, consistent, and supported are better able to lead through uncertainty without burning out or reacting in ways they later regret.

There *is* a way to hold concern and steadiness at the same time. The goal is not to create conditions where choosing help becomes more likely, and where parents don't lose themselves in the waiting.

Of course, there are moments when waiting is not appropriate. When serious safety or mental health risks emerge, parents may need to act quickly — seeking emergency care or pursuing treatment even if a teen is not yet willing. The guidance in this chapter applies to the longer arc, not to an acute crisis.

Leading With Intention Through Uncertain Times

This chapter is not a substitute for professional treatment, nor am I writing as an addiction counselor. What I offer is support for parents—grounded guidance rooted in child development and evidence-informed family approaches. My focus is not on diagnosing or treating addiction, but on how parents lead, respond, and care for themselves during a season that is emotionally demanding.

Leading with intention means shifting focus toward what parents *can* shape: the tone of communication, the consistency of boundaries, and the steadiness modeled over time. These daily choices matter, even when progress feels slow.

This kind of leadership prioritizes influence over control. It favors clarity over repeated warnings, consistency over intensity, and connection over power struggles.

Communication That Lowers Resistance

When teens feel cornered, lectured, or threatened, they often defend their behavior more strongly. In contrast, communication that lowers resistance sounds different—calmer, delivered with more care and precision, and more focused on understanding than convincing. These conversations are most effective when substance use is not actively happening, and emotions are relatively regulated. I often tell families to not engage in conversations using the acronym HALT(S)as a guide—Hungry, Angry, Lonely, Tired, or (over)Stimulated.

Here are ways you can shift conversations:

Then:

"You're ruining your future. If you don't stop, everything is going to fall apart."

Now:

"I'm worried about how this is affecting you. I'm open to talking when you are."

Then:

"I know you're lying. You always do this."

Now:

"Something doesn't feel right to me. Let's talk later when things are calmer."

Shifting to listening and connecting rather than talking at your teen is also helpful during this time. I suggest to clients that they find ways to be in the same space as their child while doing another activity, like folding laundry or working on their laptop. This makes you available to have a conversation when your teen is ready to share.

Boundaries Without Threats or Power Struggles

Many parents ask for help to set boundaries without seeming harsh. It can take practice, especially if you have taken a child-led parenting style in the past. I often role-play with parents to practice. Effective boundaries are simple, calm statements that describe what will happen, without ending in a question or inviting debate. These are not punishments. They are expressions of self-respect and, hopefully, lead a teen to better understand the consequences of their actions.

- "I'm not able to give money when substances are involved."
- "I won't cover for your missed responsibilities related to use."
- "I will step away from conversations that become unsafe or disrespectful."

Reinforcing the Behavior You Want to See

Just as important as limits is what parents choose to notice. Responsibility, honesty, effort, and sober moments are easy to overlook, but powerful when acknowledged. Reinforcement doesn't mean praise for perfection; it means recognizing steps in the right direction.

A simple "I noticed you handled that differently" or "Thank you for being honest with me" can quietly strengthen healthier patterns over time.

Together, these daily choices—how parents speak, what they allow, what they reinforce—shape the environment in which change becomes more possible.

Leading Through the Waiting

For many parents, the most painful part of this journey is the waiting—knowing help may be needed while their teen isn't ready to accept it yet. This space can feel powerless, isolating, and exhausting.

But waiting does not mean doing nothing.

This time can be used for quiet preparation, so that if your child does need professional support and is ready to engage in that work, you are steady and prepared to suggest options. That preparation might include learning about different levels of care, identifying potential providers or programs, understanding what questions to ask, and knowing what your insurance covers.

The kind of leadership discussed throughout this chapter also requires care for the parent. Self-care is not a luxury; it is part of the work. When parents are supported and regulated, they are better able to communicate thoughtfully, recover after hard moments, and stay grounded without burning out.

This kind of leadership — holding boundaries, navigating triggers, staying connected — is learnable, even in the most challenging seasons of parenting. In a culture that often minimizes marijuana use, trusting your parental intuition and choosing to lead with clarity, steadiness, and care is not overreaction; it is responsible, informed parenting. One day, your child will thank you.

Susan Notis is a certified integrative life and parent coach, award-winning educator, and bestselling co-author of *The Perfectly Imperfect Family*. She supports parents navigating emotionally complex seasons of parenting, focusing on nervous system regulation, calm communication, and steady leadership. A mother of two teenagers, Susan brings both professional expertise and lived parenting experience to her work. Her work is grounded in the belief that lasting change begins with compassion and developmentally informed leadership.

Download her free workbook, *Leading Through Teen Marijuana Dependency: A Compassionate Guide for Concerned Parents.*

THE IDENTITY THEFT YOU DIDN'T SEE COMING: HOW SMARTPHONES HIJACK WHO YOUR TEEN IS BECOMING

Dr. Carrie Mackensen

———

Kelly came to my office in despair. Her thirteen-year-old daughter, Lily, had always been a sensitive kid, but lately she was withdrawn, joyless, and unreachable. Kelly and her husband had divorced eighteen months earlier, which had been hard on everyone—but recently, things had gotten worse. Lily appeared depressed. She said she felt miserable, complained she had no friends, and seemed hopeless. Kelly tried everything to reconnect—shopping trips, hair appointments, gentle conversations—but nothing worked for more than a day or two.

When I asked about Lily's daily routine, Kelly mentioned, almost as an aside, that Lily was typically on her iPhone—social media, YouTube, games. She'd given her the phone after the divorce so they could stay in touch when Lily visited her dad's house. But now Lily was on it constantly. "It's like her only friend," Kelly said with resignation. All told, Lily was spending at least seven hours a day on her smartphone.

During my session with Lily, I asked her a question I ask every young person I work with: "What do you enjoy doing, what brings you joy?"

She sat quietly, then shrugged. She said she "didn't really know."

That answer has become alarmingly common in my practice. And it tells me something has changed among tweens and teens.

The Window That Changes Everything

Ages twelve to eighteen represent the second most critical period of brain development in any human's life, surpassed only by the first five years of life. During adolescence, the brain undergoes massive neural growth and activity while simultaneously beginning a process called pruning, which eliminates neural connections that are not being used regularly and strengthens those that are. It's the brain's version of use-it-or-lose-it. What the brain does during these years is what the brain becomes.

The developmental *task* of this period is identity formation: discovering who you are from the inside out. And your teenager is doing the critical work of individuating—separating from you just enough to form their own sense of self while still using you as their secure base. They're testing values, experimenting with interests, discovering what moves them, and building a sense of who they are that will carry them into adulthood. This work requires space—mental, emotional, and physical space—to turn inward and listen to what resonates.

Think about your own adolescence. You came home from school, and you had that space. Sure, you could call a friend on the house phone, but you couldn't constantly monitor what everyone else was doing every moment of the day. You had room to get bored. And in that boredom, you discovered things—maybe you picked up a guitar, started sketching, joined a team, wrote in a journal, or spent hours in conversation with a parent at the kitchen table. Your identity formed from the inside out, shaped by what naturally drew you in, by real experiences in a three-dimensional world, and by your relationship with the people who loved you most.

Inside Out vs. Outside In

Today's tweens and teens don't have enough of that space. Instead, they have an internet-connected device in their pocket that connects them 24/7 to their peer group, to the internet, to AI chatbots, and to algorithms designed by some of the most sophisticated engineers in the world to capture and hold their attention. Instead of identity forming from the inside out—shaped by a young person's own curiosity, talents, and relationships—it's being molded from the outside in. By what's trending. By what gets the most 'likes.' By what the algorithm serves up next. By a relentless stream of social comments and comparisons that no developing brain was designed to handle.

The average American teenager now spends over seven hours a day on screens for entertainment alone. That's seven hours when the brain is *not* building neural pathways for real-world skills, authentic relationships, and self-knowledge. And because of pruning—that use-it-or-lose-it process—the consequences are not just about wasted time. They're structural; we are talking about brain architecture here.

What does this look like in daily life? The musical instrument your child spent years learning gets abandoned in favor of scrolling. That hard-fought sport gets dropped because gaming feels easier and more immediately rewarding. The art stops. The face-to-face conversations become shorter, shallower, rarer. And the brain, doing exactly what it's designed to do, starts pruning away the neural pathways for those unused skills. The music ability. The athletic coordination. The capacity for sustained eye contact and deep conversation. The emotional attunement that only develops through *real* human connection.

Meanwhile, the pathways that *are* getting strengthened? The ones for rapid scrolling, instant gratification, external validation, and superficial social comparison.

This also affects the parent-child bond through what I call *pixelated attachment*. During this developmental stage, your child is supposed to be individuating while still orienting toward you as their primary source of connection, comfort, and guidance. But when a smartphone becomes the constant companion—the thing they reach for when they're bored, sad, confused, lonely, or hurt—that device begins to replace *you*, the parent, as that primary source. The phone becomes the go-to for emotional regulation rather than you. Your child's attachment shifts from you to a screen and the digital world. And when that happens during the exact developmental window when identity is being formed, and the brain is deciding which connections to keep and which to prune, the impact reaches far beyond screen time. It reshapes who your child is becoming and how they will relate to others for the rest of their life.

What's at Stake

Since smartphones and social media became ubiquitous with this age group, we have seen the highest rates of anxiety, depression, self-harm, and suicide in recorded history among young people. This is not a coincidence. It's what happens when developing brains are saturated with addictive technology during their most vulnerable window.

And here is what keeps me up at night as both a clinician and a mom: when today's teens are sad, confused, or emotionally overwhelmed, many of them are no longer turning to a parent. They're turning to a chatbot, a social media platform, or a stranger in an online forum. The very attachment bond that should be their anchor during these turbulent years is being eroded by the device in their pocket. Parents are being replaced, and most don't even realize it's happening.

Protecting the Space Where Identity Grows

The good news is that this is reversible—and the solution is simpler than most parents think. It doesn't require an advanced degree in technology or a complete overhaul of family life. It requires a shift in priority: choosing presence over pixels, and protecting the developmental space your child needs to become who they actually are.

Here's where to start. Delay the smartphone. Your tween or young teen does not need a portal to the entire internet in their pocket during the most vulnerable period of their brain development. If your child needs a way to reach you, give them a basic talk-and-text phone—what some call a "dumb phone"—around age fourteen. I recommend waiting until at least age sixteen for a smartphone. Those two to four years of protection give your child the space to develop a solid sense of self before the digital world has a chance to define them.

Get devices out of bedrooms. Buy your child an alarm clock. Charge phones in your bedroom closet or in the kitchen while everyone sleeps so there's no access to screens during the hours when your child should be resting—or lying in the quiet, thinking their own thoughts, which is exactly where the work of forming an identity happens.

Protect real-world connection. Encourage your child to call their friends on the phone—the actual skill of conversation is being lost to thumbs on a screen. Prioritize hobbies, sports, art, music, outdoor time, family dinners, and the kind of low-key togetherness where your teenager might actually open up to you. These are the experiences that build the neural pathways for a fulfilling, meaningful life.

This isn't about being the strictest parent on the block. It's about understanding what your child's brain needs during this window and having the courage to provide it.

The Real Child Is Still in There

Back to Lily. When her mom, at my recommendation, replaced Lily's smartphone with a basic flip phone, Lily suddenly had seven free hours in her day. Within three weeks, she was smiling again. Laughing, even.

Reconnecting with her mom and sister. Engaging with friends in the neighborhood.

With my guidance, she started journaling—and for the first time, she began processing the pain of her parents' divorce rather than numbing it with endless scrolling. She was developing real coping skills, real emotional insight.

And then something beautiful happened. Her passion for art came back.

Before the smartphone, Lily had been a phenomenal artist—charcoal, portraits, colored pencils, painting. She had a genuine talent that lit her up from the inside. But it had completely disappeared once the phone took over. Now, with the screen removed, that talent reemerged and became a core part of her identity—a source of confidence, self-expression, and genuine joy that carried her through middle school and high school.

Her mother called me, her voice full of emotion: "I feel like I got my daughter back."

The girl who couldn't answer *what do you enjoy doing?* found the answer. It had been there all along, buried under seven hours of scrolling.

Your child's real self is still in there, too. The curious, creative, capable person they are becoming doesn't need more content—they need more space. This isn't about policing your children. It's about connecting with them through your presence and protecting the environment in which they're growing up so their true selves can emerge.

Presence over pixels. That's the gift.

Dr. Carrie Mackensen—known as Dr. Carrie to her clients—is a psychologist and mom of two boys with twenty-five years of clinical experience spanning Cedars-Sinai Hospital, K-12 schools, and private practice, including serving as Clinical Director for Premier Treatment Programs. She holds a PhD in Individual, Family, and Child Psychology.

Dr. Carrie is the founder of Successful Parent and author of the forthcoming book *Digitally Dysregulated: How Screens Hijack Kids' Brains and What Parents Can Do About It*. She combines evidence-based strategies with warmth, humor, and the practical insights of a battle-tested mom. For resources and support, visit www.successfulparent.com.

SECTION FIVE

LETTING GO WHILE STAYING CLOSE

30

FROM POWER STRUGGLES TO PARTNERSHIP: THE PATH TO A BRIGHT FUTURE WITH YOUR TEEN

Coco Stanback

My son went from a happy, loving, social boy to a withdrawn, irritable, combative teen.

What happened? Who flipped the switch? It felt like just yesterday we were fine.

Every conversation felt tense. Simple things like brushing his teeth or taking a shower turned into exhausting standoffs. Homework, bedtime, and electronics felt impossible.

It didn't seem to matter what I said or how carefully I explained it. We were stuck on opposite sides, locked in a struggle neither of us knew how to win.

I was exhausted and at my wits' end.

I had a master's degree in psychology—and still, nothing I tried worked. I set clear boundaries, talked through expectations, used reasonable consequences, drafted contracts, and even tried incentives and rewards.

Instead of improving, everything escalated. More conflict. More verbal aggression. At times, physical altercations.

This was not what I imagined parenting would be like.

I was doing everything I knew to change our situation—and it was tearing us apart. I was trapped in what I now call the *illusion of control*, pouring my energy into strategies to change *him*.

Nothing shifted until I turned my attention inward. It finally dawned on me that I had it backwards. I was trying to manage him rather than myself.

When he rolled his eyes, I didn't lecture. When he snapped, I lowered my voice. When he refused, I didn't double down. I got curious instead and asked myself, *What is making this hard for him right now?*

The more I regulated myself, the less power struggle there was to fuel. Conversations began to open up, interactions softened, and little by little, the good moments started to outnumber the hard ones.

The Illusion of Control

Control doesn't come from a bad place. Most parents don't want to control their children. They want to protect them. Guide them. Keep them safe. But when emotions run high, behavior escalates, or cooperation disappears, control shows up offering relief.

It promises order. Predictability. A sense of calm. It whispers, *If you can just get this under control, everything will be fine.*

And for a while, it works.

When kids are young, control feels effective. We create routines, manage schedules, and shape their days. Almost without realizing it, we begin to equate being a good parent with being "in charge."

Over time, though, that sense of control starts to feel less solid. What once worked begins to slip—and the illusion quietly cracks.

The inner world of teens becomes more complex. Their need for autonomy increases, emotions run hotter, and friends begin to take priority. They face challenges they don't yet have the skills to handle, and their pushback can feel personal, alarming, and downright scary.

And even though we know—logically—that we can't actually control another person, we keep trying. Why?

Because fear enters the picture.

Fear that we're losing our child.

That they're drifting toward choices we can't protect them from.

That if we loosen our grip, everything will unravel.

Fear fills our heads with stories—stories that shape what we say and do in moments of stress.

It pushes us to react.

We yell. We take away the iPad, the phone, time with friends. We lecture, remind, and repeat ourselves—sometimes louder—hoping our efforts will restore order.

Not because we don't care. We're trying to protect the relationship. But fear convinces us that control will save it, when in reality, the tighter we grip, the more distance we create.

Fear lies to us about what their behavior means, what kind of child we have, and what kind of parent we need to be to fix it.

For a long time, I believed those stories. I told myself the problem was defiance—that my son was stubborn, rebellious. Those beliefs kept me stuck, convinced it was my job to change him.

The real turning point came when I let go of the beliefs I had absorbed about behavior—beliefs that divide kids into good or bad, obedient or defiant, right or wrong.

I replaced them with a different lens: that all kids want to do well, and when they don't, it's because they're struggling, not trying to be difficult.

One night, after months of fighting over bedtime, I sat at the foot of his bed and said quietly, "I don't see the world the way you do—but I want to. Help me understand."

He paused. The tension in the room eased, and for the first time in a long time, we weren't arguing—we were talking.

In that moment, our relationship softened, and a new path forward became possible.

A Different Kind of Leadership

When parents reach this point, the question is almost always the same: *If not control, then what?*

Many parents worry that letting go of control means surrendering authority. They imagine that without pressure or consequences, chaos will take over. Teenagers will run the show. Nothing will get done.

That worry makes sense, but it's based on a false choice.

The alternative to control isn't permissiveness. It's influence.

Influence is a different kind of leadership—one that becomes especially important during the teenage years, when control becomes ineffective, but guidance is still deeply needed.

This is why influence works when control no longer does. Adolescents are wired for autonomy, fairness, and emotional safety. When teens feel managed, they push back. When they feel respected and understood, they're far more open to guidance.

Over years of working with families, I've found that parents don't need more strategies to manage their teens—they need a different way of leading.

I call this framework the ARC of Influence.

ARC stands for **Attunement, Reliability, and Collaboration**—three parent-led practices that build trust, reduce power struggles, and create the conditions for meaningful change.

This shift unfolds over time. Slowly at first—more openness, fewer explosive moments, brief glimpses of cooperation. Then, through consistency, a true partnership emerges.

Seeing the Shift in Action

When Angie first reached out to me, her home was in a constant state of crisis. Her son was having multiple meltdowns a day. Mornings were especially hard—waking up, getting dressed, leaving for school—each was a battle. The intensity was so high that Angie avoided outings, worried a meltdown would erupt the moment they walked out the door—or worse, in public.

By the time we connected, Angie was exhausted, discouraged, and confused. She was doing everything she thought a "good parent" was supposed to do—and nothing was working.

Like many parents, Angie had been raised with traditional parenting approaches. She believed that consistency meant insisting that things get done, and that follow-through meant sticking to her plan and timeline. So when her son struggled, she pushed harder.

What she began to see—slowly and painfully—was that her insistence wasn't creating cooperation. It was creating escalation.

At first, shifting her perspective wasn't easy. Letting go of the belief that her son's behavior was willful or defiant felt uncomfortable—and even risky. She still worried that if she stopped insisting, things would fall apart.

Through coaching, she began to experiment with a different story. Instead of asking, "Why is he doing this to me?" she started asking, "What if this is a can't and not a won't?"

As she practiced giving her son the benefit of the doubt, something softened. She found herself pausing more often, reacting less quickly, and approaching him with greater curiosity. And as her perspective changed, so did the way she showed up with him.

With this shift, she was able to tune in to her son during difficult moments. Instead of jumping in to correct or demand, she began slowing herself down. She focused on noticing what her son might be experiencing and naming it out loud.

Sometimes that sounded like, "This feels really hard right now," or "You seem overwhelmed."

There was no fixing. No persuading. Just acknowledgment.

This didn't stop the meltdowns overnight—but it changed the emotional tone between them. Her son felt seen, not managed.

As Angie practiced attunement, she also began working on reliability. She learned to pause before reacting, even when her emotions ran high. When she raised her voice or pushed too hard—as all parents do—she took the time to repair.

She'd come back and say, "That didn't come out the way I wanted. I'm sorry. Let me try again."

Over time, her son began to trust that she wouldn't escalate or punish him for his feelings or behaviors. He felt safer bringing his big emotions to her instead of fighting against her.

Only after months of attunement and reliability did Angie and her son begin collaborating.

Together, they began to look for patterns. What made mornings harder? Which transitions were most overwhelming? What helped him stay regulated—and what made things worse?

Angie listened to her son share his experience, and she shared her concerns honestly. The solutions weren't perfect, but they were created together. They were no longer adversaries.

And gradually, things began to change.

The meltdowns that once happened daily became weekly. Then monthly. Mornings became more manageable. Leaving the house no longer felt impossible.

Today, her son is a happy, well-adjusted teenager. He's doing well in school and is involved in sports and community activities. She recently told me, "I'm having so much fun raising my teenage son; I never thought I'd be able to say that."

Challenges still come up—as they do in all families—but Angie no longer feels trapped in a cycle of control and conflict.

She learned something powerful: influence didn't come from insisting harder.

It came from leading differently.

When It Feels Hard

When parents begin shifting from control to influence, almost every parent I work with says some version of the same thing:

"I understand it in theory—but in the moment, I just react."

And that makes sense.

When emotions run high, control feels faster and more familiar.

Along with the struggle come persistent doubts:

If I stop insisting, will things fall apart?

If I soften, will I lose authority?

What if this doesn't work?

Those doubts don't mean you're failing. They mean you're stretching.

The shift doesn't happen in grand gestures. It happens in small, imperfect moments—pausing when you want to react, repairing when you stumble, staying curious when you want to clamp down. Progress isn't linear, but every attempt builds trust.

A Relationship That Lasts a Lifetime

Influence is powerful—but easy to overlook when control feels so convincing. Control pulls us into a constant tug-of-war where someone wins, and someone loses.

Influence follows a different arc.

It begins with attunement—slowing down enough to validate our child's experience. That builds reliability. Our kids learn they can count on us to be steady and fair. From there, collaboration becomes possible. We stop working against our kids and start working with them. That's where influence grows.

I know this not just as a coach, but as a parent. Over time, the battles with my son gave way to conversations. We've learned how to stay connected even when we don't agree. Today, he regularly calls to talk through ideas, ask for my perspective, and share what's happening in his world. The power struggles that once defined us have been replaced by mutual respect, trust, and love.

As I write this, our favorite NFL team is headed to the Super Bowl— and my grown son is taking me, his *mom.* It's a gift that reminds me how far we've come, one I hold with deep gratitude.

As you move forward, notice the seeds of influence that may already be present. Where are you attuning, showing up reliably, and collaborating with your child?

And if you don't see much evidence yet, that's okay. You know where to begin. Start with one moment. One pause. One curious question.

Because in the end, every parent wants a relationship that lasts a lifetime.

Coco Stanback is the founder of Heart 4 Kids Coaching, a parent coach, speaker, and Certified Collaborative & Proactive Solutions (CPS) provider. With over 15 years of experience supporting families—and a decade immersed in the CPS model—she helps parents move from power struggles to partnership by choosing influence over control. Coco equips families with practical, compassionate tools to build trust, strengthen connection, and create lasting change. To continue exploring these ideas, download her free guide, *The ARC of Influence: A Practical Guide to Building Lifelong Connection*, https://heart-4kids.lpages.co/arcofinfluence/, and explore coaching and resources at Heart4KidsCoaching.com.

WHEN CONTROL STOPS WORKING: REBUILDING YOUR FAMILY'S ARCHITECTURE OF TRUST

Debbie Simmons

If control works so well when children are young, why does it fail when they need us most? I did not ask that until the night I realized I was losing my teenager while doing everything right.

It did not happen all at once. There was no defining argument, no dramatic moment. It was quieter. A growing awareness that the teenager I loved was still under my roof, and yet slowly becoming unreachable.

They were not rebellious or cruel. They were simply distant. And that distance hurt more than any broken rule ever could.

Like most parents, I did what had always worked. I set boundaries. I followed through. I explained. I enforced. I exhausted every strategy I knew. Still, something felt unstable beneath the surface. I was doing everything right and still losing influence. The problem was not behavior. It was structure.

If nothing changes, distance does not stay quiet. It hardens into silence, resentment, and eventually estrangement.

The Authority Shift No One Teaches

Every family is built on authority, and every form of authority is carried by a structure. When children are young, that structure comes from us. Having limits and healthy boundaries, thoughtfully observing our kids, allowing kids to experience the natural consequences of their actions, and providing adult guidance are needed.

But teenagers are not children in training. They are adults in formation. Neuroscience confirms that the brain is remodeling during adolescence. Reward systems accelerate. Emotional reactivity intensifies. The regions responsible for judgment and impulse control are still under construction. Control collapses not because teens are defiant, but because their brains are wired for independence before wisdom is complete.

When the system does not grow, pressure builds. We try to carry a maturing soul inside a structure built for dependence, and the weight eventually exceeds what it can hold. This is when control collapses, because the structure is no longer designed for the season it is serving.

Adolescence is the bridge where authority must be rebuilt, not enforced. What replaces control is not chaos. It must be architected. Trust is not assumed. It is built. At its core, trust is built on love that chooses presence over power.

When Control Collapses

Most families respond by tightening their grip. They explain more, monitor more, enforce more, and hope effort will compensate for misalignment. But the harder they push, the further away their teenagers drift. When teens pull away, they are not rejecting their parents. They are protecting themselves. Withdrawal is not rebellion. It signals that the system no longer feels safe for growth.

A father once told me, "Nothing is wrong in our house. We just feel tired all the time." His son was doing well. No red flags. No blowups. But the family lived on edge. If he stayed calm, things worked. If he pulled back, the system felt like it might collapse. This was not a behavior issue. It was a trust issue. The family relied on his emotional energy instead of a shared structure.

What teens need is not more control. They need a structure strong enough to hold both truth and trust.

From Parenting to Architecture

This is not a method or a set of tips. It is a way of thinking about what holds a family together when the old structures stop. This is where the Architecture of Trust was born. Not as a parenting style, but as a trust system. What we call behavior problems are structural failures, and structure, not effort, determines whether a family can grow through change.

Rebuilding authority does not mean removing boundaries. It means relocating their purpose, from managing behavior to shaping character. Structure without relationship becomes rigid. Relationship without structure becomes unsafe. Trust is the architecture that holds them together. Discipline is the loving construction of limits that protect what matters most. Authority does not disappear in adolescence. It matures.

The Inner Shift That Makes Trust Possible

This work requires an inner shift. Control is fueled by fear of loss. Trust begins when we release ownership of who our teenager must become and choose to mentor who they are becoming.

Parents must move from emotional managers to emotional coaches, helping teens name, regulate, and navigate their inner world instead of correcting it. Trust grows when teens feel emotionally understood, not emotionally corrected.

Trust grows when parents model emotional courage. Naming fear, owning mistakes, and staying present reshape the emotional climate. Trust does not remove authority. It transforms it.

You do not rebuild by trying harder. You rebuild by surrendering what was never meant to carry this weight alone.

The Blueprint for Rebuilding Trust

Once parents understand the issue is structural, the question becomes simple and unsettling. How do we rebuild what is no longer holding?

Over time, I noticed a rhythm in families who felt stuck. It was not a technique. It was a pattern of response. I named this rhythm **T.R.U.S.T.**

It begins when you **T – Take inventory**, not of your teenager's behavior, but of your own inner response. You notice what rises when conversations go sideways and what you are trusting to hold the relationship.

From there, you **R – Replace the default.** You question whether what you have been trusting still serves this season. You choose responses that are intentional rather than automatic.

As those choices repeat, they form rhythm. This is where you **U – Use simple systems**, small, dependable anchors that hold when emotions rise. Predictable moments of connection. Clear ways to repair.

But systems only work when they are named. This is when you **S – Say it out loud.** You clarify what matters and how your family handles stress. You let your teenager hear that this is not about control. It is about connection.

And finally, you **T – Test and tweak.** You notice what holds and what cracks under pressure. You adjust without shame.

This is how trust becomes a tool instead of an assumption.

When Trust Becomes Real

Sarah came to me exhausted. Her fifteen-year-old daughter, Lily, had done nothing wrong, but tension filled their home. Conversations ended in silence. Every question felt like an interrogation.

When we slowed down, Sarah realized she was reacting out of fear. Each time Lily pulled away, panic drove her to push harder. What she trusted was urgency.

Once she saw it, she replaced the default. The next time Lily shut down, Sarah paused. She let the moment breathe.

Over the next few weeks, Sarah created small rhythms. Short check-ins. Simple moments of connection. She named the shift. She told Lily she was not trying to control her. She was trying to stay connected.

The change was not dramatic. But it was real. Lily began talking again, not because she had to, but because she felt safe.

That is what rebuilding trust looks like.

The Legacy We Are Choosing

How we cross this bridge will shape whether our children return to us when life gets hard, trust us with their children, and carry our voice forward. This is not about today's tension. It is about tomorrow's relationship.

I held control longer than I should have. I protected a structure that had already expired, and it cost me closeness before I understood why. That is when this became a calling, not a message. Fear-based authority was the only model many of us were given. Trust transforms authority.

Success is not perfect behavior. It is adult children who want to come home, who trust our counsel, and who choose relationship when they no longer need permission.

If time feels short, hear this. It is not too late. Even small shifts rebuild bridges faster than you think.

Pause. Place your hand over your heart. Notice where fear has been leading instead of love. Surrender what you were never meant to carry alone.

This is not about fixing your family. It is about becoming the kind of presence your family can trust.

Debbie Simmons is a faith-driven keynote speaker, author, CEO of Anchor Point, and a leadership strategist known as *The Legacy Architect*. She helps high-capacity leaders who feel successful but quietly unfulfilled build legacies that outlive their titles. As the creator of the *Architecture of Trust*™, she is the originator of trust architecture for leadership and family systems, revealing what is truly shaping behavior and realigning foundations for lasting impact. Debbie speaks globally to audiences seeking transformational leadership rooted in purpose, courage, and faith. Her work bridges neuroscience, emotional intelligence, and Kingdom principles to create sustainable influence and legacy-driven growth.

TETHERED TEEN: YOU HAVE TO LET YOUR TEEN GO, BUT THEY DON'T HAVE TO LEAVE YOU

Jennifer Lytle

Up to 30% of adult children are now low- or no-contact with their parents. That number should matter to every parent of a teen because the tether that keeps your child connected to you isn't built after they leave—it's built now. One day, you will let them go. Will they come back? That's the real gauge of your work.

Building the Tether

Parents find their way to me after trying everything they can think of to better manage their teen—cutting social media, switching schools, tightening the reins. But pulling your teen closer through control often pushes them further away. What works is building a tether.

Your teen is designed to go farther than you can, naturally beyond your reach. It's what you've been working so diligently to support. Today's parents don't just plan for releasing adolescents—they anticipate and accommodate a perpetual invitation for return landings through a secure tether. Or at least they should.

Three Core Principles of the TETHER Framework

The TETHER Framework rests on three principles: **position**, **pace**, and **posture**. Position is where you stand—moving from center stage to supporting cast. Pace is speed—matching your teen's rhythm rather than forcing yours. Posture is how you show up—humble enough to be wrong, open enough to learn from them.

These principles aren't sequential, and you don't need all three at once. If they feel overwhelming, pick one. Try it for a week. Journal what you notice. Decide if you can try a second principle simultaneously or independently. Adaptability may prove the winning strategy with teens.

This works even if you have multiple children—especially then, because each child needs a different kind of tether.

Position

Position means shifting from center stage to supporting cast—close enough to matter, far enough to let them move in a direction of their choosing. It's the hardest principle to adopt for parents who've spent years being their child's gravitational center.

One family I worked with learned this the hard way.

Brent started skipping school, basically walking straight out the back door the minute he was dropped off on school grounds. After ultimatums, temporary eviction, and a broken family contract, Brent's parents decided to change their approach because hovering wasn't working. They instead engaged in family counseling using the TETHER Framework.

What Brent's parents discovered—and what I see repeatedly in my practice—is that relinquishing the starring role in your child's life doesn't mean abandoning the production. They shifted from control to mentor, from center-stage star to supporting cast. They were still essential. They just stopped directing every scene. In fact, they found that a teacher could better mentor their son, inspiring a new-found interest in 4H and competitive shows, something they knew little about. Even though Brent continued to struggle somewhat with grades, he was motivated to complete the show season and was more responsible with class attendance. Because someone outside of the family dynamic affected outcome.

Position maintains perfect distance. Too close, and there is no movement. Too distant, and the movement is unwieldy.

It's a special season when our children are deeply attached to us. As the conscientious parent holding this book, you have already begun to pivot. Far from "quitting" parenting, you will step into a new role. Your teen's development still requires your presence and attunement. No longer are you the centrifugal force in your teen's life. It is deeply important that you have helped to build, and equipped your teen to build, a community of their own—one in which they no longer count on you alone to maintain connections on their behalf. This is the power of position.

What this looks like in practice: Sign up for a youth organization like a scouting group or a local church youth group. Volunteer so you can be involved without taking on the responsibility for your teen. Promote annual activities, such as summer camp or a sports league, so your teen can build deep relationships over time. Encourage houseovers where your teen and friends can gather to game, celebrate, or watch movies. Make it fun, but don't make it about your fun by moving center stage. Tethering your teen to the outside community establishes them. It's a baton well passed—and isn't that what you're after?

Pace

Pace is what keeps the tether from snapping. Pull too hard, too fast, and you lose the connection. Some teens need you to slow down. Others are ready to move faster than you're comfortable with.

Regina learned this after years of resistance from her son Matt. Regina was a goer. If she wasn't going, she wasn't living. She couldn't understand why Matt didn't operate the way she did. Tension flared up occasionally, but when Matt quit baseball his sophomore year of high school, Regina ratcheted it up by accusing Matt of giving up and forfeiting any decent future. Matt was unable to share that he had known for years that baseball was not his sport. He was in it for her. He didn't want to disappoint her, but he said he "couldn't take it anymore" and asked if he could live with his out-of-state dad. It took almost a year before Regina was able to honestly try out, both verbally and in practice, "I'm doing less, better." For Regina, this was a hard shift after growing up with a perspective that she was perpetually missing out. When Matt moved with his dad, she was finally willing to change.

Matt needed his mother to ease off the throttle. But pace cuts both ways—sometimes your teen is ready before you are.

Take the case of Valorie, who requested an urgent appointment for her early tween daughter, Vera. Vera had been asking about body parts and using language that Valorie had never used. She was initially afraid her daughter might be developing an unhealthy fixation, but Vera was simply repeating terms she had picked up at school. Shame wasn't yet part of her curiosity. Once Valorie recognized her daughter's innocent interest, she was willing to have factual conversations about human sexuality. It came much too soon for Valorie's preference, but she was willing to face her discomfort to meet the pace needs of her daughter.

Whether your teen needs you to speed up or slow down, pace is about reading their rhythm—not imposing yours.

What this looks like in practice: Does your pre-teen or teen need a little bit of adventure? Try an arcade game outing. Maybe you sense your teen needs a break from a hectic pace? Choose an activity to purposefully play hooky from, like Sunday morning church. Perhaps a tiny dose of quality time is all you can afford? Make a tradition of Wednesday morning donuts or start an annual parent-teen date night. It's not just about the activity—it's about your pace when together. This can show up with an observation like, "I noticed you took the time to share your experience today." It may be a reminder: "I'm so glad to be with you, right now!"

Posture

Posture is how you show up—humble, curious, willing to be wrong. It's the hardest principle for parents who've earned their expertise the hard way.

I learned this in my own kitchen.

"Who cares about Legos?!" I bellowed in an impatient fit. This was in response to my teen complaining about how I favor the youngest. This only served to validate his second complaint that I "never listen" to him. I needed to shut it (my mouth, that is) before my teen son shut me out.

Thinking better of the situation, I tried again. "I'm sorry. I might not care about Legos, but I do care about you. When it happens again," I slowed down to give my words weight, "when you feel like I'm not listening to you, please, can you tell me about it?" I don't want you to feel that way. And I don't want to do that to you."

We didn't resolve the Lego issue, but we did maintain the tether's security during that conversation.

We are going to blow it. It's not going to be the right time; you're going to be worried about something that hasn't happened yet. It simply cannot be avoided. What matters is what happens next. Purposeful and sincere apologies are requisite to any relationship of real value. Saying you're sorry and admitting you were wrong can be a significant step towards connection.

That's particularly true when you have a teen who is ready to rule the world and a parent (you) who has gleaned years of lessons and insights. You know a lot. But guess what: your teen has insight too. This is part of the transition. It's a different world out here today.

We've landed on foreign soil, and your teen knows today better than you might—at least about *some* things. Acceptance of your teen's divergent worldview, appreciation for their "insider knowledge" about all things modern, and acknowledgment of your own limitations—all of this offers a freedom in the relationship for both you and your teen to show up with individual value, confidence, curiosity, and openness. It's this humble openness that fosters connection. Real, long-lasting, come-back-just-because kind of connection.

What this looks like in practice: "That's a different way to go about it! Glad you showed me." Permission granted to laugh with: "Wow. You have the most unique way of looking at things! I learn a lot from you." And you won't get any objections to: "You are so fun"—spotlighting your teen's contribution.

The Tether Holds

Your teen may sigh, roll their eyes, or answer in monosyllables. That's not failure—that's adolescence. The tether holds even as they pull away.

Remember that 30% statistic? Those relationships didn't rupture overnight. They frayed slowly, through years of control instead of connection, through pace that never matched, through posture that wouldn't bend.

Your job isn't to keep them close. It's to make sure they can find their way back.

Jennifer Lytle is a Licensed Marriage and Family Therapist and the founder of Joyful Journeys Counseling. She specializes in evidence-based treatment for anxiety and has worked with families in clinical settings since 2017. Her work has been featured by NBC, Austin Fit Magazine, and Texas Today. She serves as the Austin Chapter President with Christian Counselors of Texas, providing education and training for counselors. Follow her at joyfuljourneyscounseling.com and get her three communication tools for connecting through conflict-free conversations, even about difficult topics.

PARENTING NEURODIVERGENT TEENS: BALANCING SUPPORT AND BUILDING AUTONOMY

Lisa Lottatore-French, Psy.D., BCBA-D

As parents of neurodiverse children, we have long histories of fighting for our kids and advocating for their needs. We are Mama Bears and Papa Bears to our core. We have prompted our children through things that usually come naturally to neurotypical children. We have watched them struggle, and we have always been there to support them as they worked through temper tantrums or learned new skills. So how do we make that shift from knowing what our child needs and wanting to help them as much as we can, to helping them become independent teens on their way to adulthood? We start to recognize that, as teenagers, our neurodiverse children are also going to go through all the regular developmental struggles. They need to try things on their own and make mistakes so they can learn and grow. We have to put our Mama Bear and Papa Bear selves aside and trust that everything we have taught them will get them through this next phase of life. Way easier said than done, right?

When my son was three, I sat in a room full of specialists and watched as the psychologist, speech therapist, occupational therapist, physical therapist, special education preschool team, and neurologist conducted assessments of him. I listened as they told me the things he couldn't do, and might never would, and I set out to prove them wrong. I focused on getting him the therapies I could, getting him into the right classes at school, and working with him at home as much as he could tolerate while still making it fun. I briefly thought about the teen years, but my focus was on day-to-day progress and developmental milestones: speech, making friends, potty training. His becoming a teenager seemed so far off.

Fast forward twelve years, and I feel like I only blinked twice, and he is now fifteen and taller than my 5'5" self. Now that he's a teen, I feel a different crunch—a new kind of urgency. Choosing your battles at three is different from choosing them at fifteen, when you know time is precious, and you want to help him toward adulthood. Questions I'd pushed aside when he was a toddler came flooding back: "Will he be able to live independently?" "Will he be able to make his own medical or financial decisions?" "Do I need to get legal guardianship or conservatorship for him?" "What will happen to him after his dad and I are gone?"

These questions made me wonder whether I was doing too much for him and whether I was challenging him enough. I re-evaluate his goals, his services, the whole picture. And then I was hit with grief again. The same grief that surfaced every time friends who had babies at the same time were sharing about their child excelling at a sport, getting on the honor roll, moving on to high school, and soon driving, dating, prom, college applications—and I was just wondering if he would forever be living at home under my care. But lately, the grief has become a catalyst to recognize all the things my son can do. I have enjoyed learning about his special interests, watching him excel at things, and developing his unique personality.

If I was wondering these things—with years of clinical training behind me—I knew other parents were wrestling with the same questions. Here's what I've learned, both as a psychologist and as a mom, about navigating this stage.

Neurodiversity looks so different for everyone. I had to learn and understand my son's unique profile. His way of processing information, regulating emotions, and how he communicated his needs looked different from those of neurotypical children. This helped me realize that autonomy looks so different for neurodiverse teens, and I had to consider his underlying cognitive, social-emotional, or motor planning difficulties while identifying his autonomy goals. I also started to recognize burnout, masking, and demand avoidance if we pushed too much. What helped me was choosing three tasks that would make my day run more smoothly if my son could do them independently. Then I **broke** those tasks down into steps and forward-chained them until he could do the task independently. For example, when teaching my son how to take a shower, I broke down each step because I had to teach him in order, or he would forget a step. Some other tasks I did this with were brushing teeth, getting dressed, doing laundry, making a bowl of cereal, and using the microwave to heat up food. I plan to do the same when teaching him how to go grocery shopping, order and pay for food at restaurants, arrange transportation to appointments, etc.

Scaffolding is a concept I use every day, both in my practice and at home. It means providing temporary, structured support while your teen learns a new skill—then gradually stepping back as they show they're ready. It reduces anxiety, keeps them on task, and builds genuine confidence because they're doing it themselves, with you as a safety net rather than a driver. Visual schedules, checklists, and reminders are a good starting point. But the real power comes from co-planning—sitting down with your teen and asking what *they* feel is important to learn. When they have a voice in setting goals and timelines, their investment changes completely. Sometimes what helps most is simply being there. Body doubling—being present in the room while your teen works through a task—can be surprisingly effective. You're not directing, just offering your quiet presence as an anchor.

For social situations, practice helps enormously. Role-play everyday conversations, practice small talk, rehearse how to navigate a disagreement with a friend. These aren't scripts your teen memorizes—they're rehearsals that build muscle memory. I have had to role-play socially appropriate boundaries with my son. For example, using curse words is very typical among teenagers, but we had some incidents in which he had to learn what is more appropriate to say around peers, not necessarily around adults or people in authority.

The hardest question for most parents when scaffolding is when to step back. There's no universal timeline. Fade supports based on readiness, not age. And keep checking: Is your support helping or becoming a crutch? Are you jumping in before they've had a chance to try? Adjust as you go.

Teaching my teenager autonomy through co-regulation is another concept I use while building autonomy. Learning self-regulation will help your teenager manage their emotions and impulses, adapt to new situations, be more flexible with change, and feel more confident in daily interactions. I had to work on modeling emotional regulation in real time and recognizing my own nervous system responses. Your teen will learn self-regulation through practice, so it's important that you model calm behavior and problem-solving strategies in the moment when a stressful situation arises. Labeling your emotion "I'm feeling sad that our plans were changed," or "I'm feeling nervous about visiting a new school" will help your teen start to label their own emotions. I also model taking a deep breath or saying that I need a break or need time to think about an action plan.

Co-regulation also includes acknowledging that your feelings were hurt, taking responsibility for saying something hurtful, and apologizing for making a mistake. This can help restore a feeling of safety and calm, and then talk about what you could have done instead, or what you plan to do next time. This will help build trust and connection with your teenager and model how to repair their own relationships if something happens with their own friends. Also, creating action plans during calm times will help them know what to say or do when tempers flare or when they find themselves in stressful situations.

Last, as we are preparing our neurodivergent teens for adulthood, remember that everyone is on their own timeline, and that's OK! Sit down with your teen and have early discussions about their own life goals and what is important to them. Do they want to attend college, get a job, have romantic relationships, or live on their own? Discuss work environments, career goals, and whether any accommodations will be needed to be successful. In my practice, I encounter a lot of families who did not keep documentation of their child's ADHD or Autism diagnosis, and this was a barrier to getting the appropriate support when taking college classes, applying for jobs, or applying for disability programs. I keep all of his assessments and school records in a folder, as well as digital copies in an email folder, so they are accessible to him in the future.

Teach and encourage self-advocacy across environments so that your teen can request help when needed or recognize when someone is trying to take advantage of them. Keep in mind that we all continue to need support from our family and friends as we go through life. Our neurodivergent teens are no different. You may observe regression during transitions, and at other times, they seem to be growing up too fast! It's important to continue being their safe home base for when they need additional support.

As your teenager approaches adulthood, continue to celebrate their strengths and accomplishments. Remind them that neurological differences such as autism, ADHD, learning differences, and sensory processing differences are normal variations of the human brain. I remind my son that neurodivergence is *not* something to fix. I think of my son as being a star-shaped peg, and if I tried to smash him into a circular hole, I would damage all those star tips that make him shine. So, let's continue to support our neurodivergent teens in being their authentic selves, as they build autonomy and feel supported, respected, and trusted.

Lisa Lottatore-French, Psy.D., BCBA-D, is a licensed psychologist and Board Certified Behavior Analyst specializing in autism spectrum disorders, ADHD, and developmental and behavioral health challenges. With more than 20 years of experience in diagnostics, treatment planning, behavior therapy, parent training, and supervision, she is passionate about helping families balance meaningful support with the intentional building of autonomy. As both a clinician and mother of three teenagers, including a neurodivergent child, Dr. French brings personal insight to empowering children to grow with confidence and independence—because the ultimate goal is raising humans who don't need you for everything... but still choose to text you back.

SUPPORTING YOUR TEEN'S EMERGING IDENTITY

Sheryl Ang

The first time my teenager rolled his eyes and walked away mid-sentence, I felt a door slam shut. Where was the child who used to tell me everything? What I've learned—both as a parent and as a coach—is that this painful moment marks the beginning of something essential: your teen is becoming their own person. The question isn't whether they'll pull away; that's developmentally necessary. The question is whether we can stay close enough to help them make sense of who they're becoming.

During adolescence, the brain undergoes a massive reorganization. Teens aren't being difficult for the sake of being difficult—they're literally rewiring. This process drives them to question everything, including us. The parents they once idolized now appear deeply flawed. This is normal. This is necessary. And how we respond shapes not just our relationship, but their emerging sense of self.

Imagine being thirteen again. You are physically, emotionally, and mentally changing. You see paradox, hypocrisy, even injustice, and fully experience the depths of emotions—sadness, fear, rage. You start to see the parents you have idolized for years as deeply flawed, like a broken vase. You didn't ask for this, but your brain simply changes. When your world is turned upside down, these behaviors all make sense. The only way to cope is to question everything. Including your parents.

The Fear No One Talks About

What if my teen comes away from this "brain upgrade" believing they can no longer trust me for help?

This is the fear that haunts many parents of teens: What if, when the dust settles, they don't want us in their lives? Beyond managing a teen's rollercoaster emotions, what I'm most afraid of is losing a place in their heart. Lively conversations and laughter that fill the hallway now could be replaced by distant, perfunctory ones.

I'm not ready to meet my fate with sighs of resignation. I don't believe disconnection is the only way. Over the years, I've discovered something that changed how I parent: *how* we help teens interpret their experiences shapes the identity they form. When we help them make meaning of what happens to them, we don't just preserve connection—we help them become who they're meant to be.

How Identity Forms

Here's how it works. Say your teen's friend group excludes him from a hangout. He comes home hurt and confused. In that moment, he's not just processing what happened—he's deciding what it *means*. He might conclude: *I'm not valued because they abandoned me.* Or he might think: *They had a bad day; this says nothing about my worth.* Or he might decide it's inconsequential and move on.

Whichever interpretation he lands on, similar experiences will reinforce it. Over time, that initial belief hardens into identity. The teen who decided he was abandoned might become someone who's cautious around friends—not as a choice, but as who he believes he *is*.

Research confirms what many parents sense intuitively: when we help children navigate the meaning-making component of their experiences, they form a healthier sense of self and have better mental health. When parents stay present as a guiding light during this time, making meaning together, teens have a higher chance of forming healthy beliefs about themselves.

But What If They Won't Talk to Me?

Before I share how to have these conversations, let's address reality: What happens when my teen responds with single-word answers? When all I see is eye rolls, side stares, and walking away mid-conversation?

Take heart. Expect resistance—and know that this is less about disrespect than growing autonomy. Taking it personally derails you from your bigger objective: helping them develop healthy belief systems. And teens can sniff hidden teaching agendas from miles away.

Positioning matters. Talking side-by-side feels safer than sitting across from each other—it's less confrontational. Invite them to share more: "Tell me more." "What happened first... then what?" And try going sideways—instead of direct questions about their situation, ask about someone else's. "What would you do if you were him?" You can also narrate a situation aloud, letting them watch you troubleshoot in real time.

When they do engage—even briefly—you'll want tools ready. In my coaching practice, I've identified three patterns that help parents support healthy identity formation.

Three Pathways to Healthy Identity

The teen who can speak their truth. This identity forms when a teen learns to listen to their inner wisdom and express themselves without fear. It develops when parents help them make meaning of what they're experiencing—building emotional vocabulary, validating feelings, and creating space for their voice.

What this sounds like in practice:

- "When he said that to you, what emotions did you notice?"

- "No wonder you felt so much rage—I would feel that too."

- "Did you believe what he said was really true?"

- "If this means a lot to you, I wonder what other ways you could express it so you'd be heard?"

Over time, these conversations help your teen form the belief *I matter*, which consolidates into an identity: *I'm someone who can express what matters to me.*

The teen who can navigate conflict. This identity forms when teens learn to read the room and work through difficult conversations without fighting or surrendering their values. When parents help teens manage emotions and see multiple perspectives, they support the development of lasting relationships over herd mentality.

What this sounds like in practice:

- "I see this is so hard. I'm here for you."

- "Did you notice what he was feeling?"

- "What would help keep the group together and moving forward?"

- "The way you handled that showed me you can navigate difficult conversations."

Over time, your teen forms the belief *conflict doesn't mean friendship is over*, which consolidates into: *I'm someone who can navigate difficult conversations.*

The teen who can pursue what matters. This identity emerges when a teen is drawn to producing something meaningful—a project, a product, a process, an idea. When parents serve as a sounding board rather than a director, teens develop an inner compass and the determination to realize their dreams.

What this sounds like in practice:

- "What could possibly go wrong here? Are you willing to accept those risks?"

- "This is hard. Would it help to think back to a time you found the strength to work through something difficult?"
- "What story do you form of yourself when you choose to take this on? Is it from a place of conviction, or from a place of fear?"

Over time, your teen forms the belief *uncertainty is tolerable*, which consolidates into: *I'm someone who can follow through.*

While these conversations may sound like "just asking questions," it's the embodiment of presence, attunement, and validation—the very same qualities we want our teens to have—that truly shifts the needle. When we show up this way, we reposition ourselves from commanders to respected companions tackling life together.

When It Gets Harder

Sometimes, though, asking the right questions isn't enough. The teen's reaction runs deeper than the moment itself.

My client Anna has a teen who was constantly irritated and angry with everyone. Every time she was asked to do something—even something small, like sorting laundry—she became rude and hostile. It looked like defiance. It felt like disrespect. But what was really happening was something more complicated: her daughter was caught in an inner dilemma.

She felt trapped. Either she complies and trades her needs for love, acceptance, and connection—or she resists to preserve her autonomy. The tension between obedience and independence was too painful to hold, so it exploded out as anger.

This is when we help unpack the dilemma. Life isn't black or white, but shades of grey. When Anna said to her daughter, "If you were able to find time to sort the laundry at your own pace, would that meet both our needs and make you less angry?"—she was modeling something powerful: how to preserve your values and preferences while staying in connection with others.

The shift was subtle but real. Anna's daughter began to see herself differently. Not *I'm a bad teen who can't do what I'm told*, but *I'm a responsible but tired teen who needs some control over my time*. That's identity change—and it happened because Anna helped her daughter find a new meaning for her experience.

The Paradox

The ultimate paradox of this work is this: despite all our efforts, we still have to let go of any attachment to our teen's eventual choices. We can only influence and shape—not control or dictate. Even though we're hardwired to fix and protect, tying our own identity to our teen's life choices is a recipe for disaster.

Let situations unfold. Don't offer suggestions first. When teens feel we're not trying to control them, they're far more likely to let us in. And that's when the real work—the meaning-making, the identity-shaping—becomes possible.

Sheryl Ang is a bestselling co-author, therapeutic coach, and founder of Self Directed Life. A former finance executive turned homeschooling mother of three, Sheryl brings both professional insight and personal experience to families navigating adolescence. She works with parents through individual coaching and group programs, helping them break reactive patterns and build lasting connection with their teens. If you'd like support putting these ideas into practice, download the free guide via the QR code below. Or connect with Sheryl on IG @selfdirectedsheryl

LEADING WITH LOVE

Stephanie Brill

I was sitting across from a mother in my office, a woman who had driven three hours from a small farming community to see me, when she said something I have never forgotten: "I love my daughter more than anything in this world. I just don't know how to love this part of her."

That question, in various forms, is the one I have heard most often in my two decades of working with families of gender-diverse and LGBTQ young people. Parents who love their children deeply, who would do anything for them, but who feel lost when their child's identity leads them into unfamiliar territory.

Maybe your child has told you directly that they are gay, or that they feel like a different gender than you expected. Maybe you have noticed patterns that have you wondering. Or maybe you are simply trying to learn more before a conversation you are not sure how to have.

Wherever you are starting from, here is the most important thing I can tell you: your love and support are the most significant factors in your child's wellbeing. When LGBTQ young people have families that remain loving and connected, they thrive. They build meaningful relationships, pursue fulfilling lives, and achieve mental health outcomes comparable to those of their peers. Family support is not just helpful. It is protective. It can be lifesaving.

You do not need to have all the answers. You do not need to understand everything right away. Many loving parents hold traditional or religious beliefs and still find ways to stay close to their children. What matters most is that your child knows your love for them is not conditional, that you are not going anywhere, no matter who they are.

Understanding the Landscape

One of the first things I help parents understand is that there are three separate aspects of identity that often get tangled together: gender identity, gender expression, and sexual orientation. Understanding these distinctions often eases confusion.

Gender identity is our internal sense of self in regard to gender. It is who we know ourselves to be on the inside, whether that is a boy, a girl, both, neither, or something else entirely. Gender identity is not a choice, and it cannot be changed. Most children develop a stable sense of their gender identity early in life, though for some, this understanding clarifies later, especially in adolescence.

Gender expression is how we present ourselves to the world through clothing, hairstyle, interests, and activities. Expression is more fluid than identity and can change over time and across contexts. Importantly, gender expression does not determine gender identity or sexual orientation. A boy who enjoys dresses may grow up to be straight and cisgender. A girl with short hair may be fully comfortable with her assigned gender.

Sexual orientation refers to who we are attracted to emotionally, romantically, or physically. Like gender identity, it is an innate part of who we are. Nothing you did or did not do caused your child's sexual orientation.

For many young people, awareness of sexual orientation unfolds gradually. Some notice early differences in their feelings, even if they lack words for them. Others do not recognize their attractions until puberty, when romantic and sexual feelings become more apparent. Some do not fully understand their orientation until adulthood. All of these paths are normal.

For many teens, gender and sexuality are intertwined parts of their journey. Some young people are sorting through questions about both who they are and who they are attracted to, sometimes at the same time. This is not confusion. It reflects the complexity of identity development.

Sexual orientation is about attraction to others. Gender identity is about who your child is inside. When we confuse the two, we often make assumptions that have little to do with who our children actually are. Untangling these distinctions helps young people and parents make sense of their experience.

What Your Child Needs Now

Your child may be confused, or they may be certain. They may be struggling, or they may feel proud. What you are seeing may be a period of exploration, or it may reflect a lifelong truth. The reality is that neither you nor your child can know this with certainty at the outset.

What you can know is that your child is doing the developmental work of figuring out who they are, which is exactly what adolescents are meant to do.

The culture of your family and community will shape how your child experiences this part of themselves. When young people fear rejection from the people they love most, they may hide or struggle in silence. When they know they are loved and accepted, they can explore their identity from a place of safety rather than fear. You have more influence over which of these paths your child walks than anyone else in their life.

It can be hard to watch your child sit with uncertainty, and it is tempting to want answers. But your child does not need you to predict their future. They need you to be present with them now.

Research consistently shows that family support is the most influential factor in an LGBTQ young person's well-being. When families provide strong support, LGBTQ youth have mental health outcomes comparable to their peers. When young people experience their families as hostile or dismissive of who they are, the risks of depression, substance use, and self-harm increase significantly.

I have seen this play out many times. I have watched families who began in uncertainty become their child's greatest source of strength.

I have also sat with young people whose early family responses left wounds that took years to heal. What made the difference was rarely the parents' beliefs. It was whether the child felt loved through the uncertainty.

When children feel secure in their family's love, they are better able to navigate stress, take healthy risks, and recover from setbacks. Feeling loved does not remove challenges, but it gives young people the resilience to face them.

Supporting your LGBTQ child does not require abandoning your values. It means continuing to show your love and staying connected.

I think of a father I worked with who told me, after months of struggle, "I still don't fully understand it. But I realized my job isn't to understand first. It's to love. The understanding can come later." What stayed with me was not that his questions disappeared, but that he stopped letting them stand between him and his child. Once love led the way, everything else became easier to navigate.

Practical Ways to Show Support

Stay connected. LGBTQ young people may pull away if they fear rejection, especially during adolescence, when distance from parents can already feel like part of growing up. Make intentional efforts to remain close, and let your child know you are available, even when they do not seem interested in talking.

Listen more than you talk. Your child has often been thinking about this longer than you have, and they may be sharing only part of what they are feeling at first. Before responding with advice or concern, make sure you understand what they are actually telling you.

Use their name and pronouns. If your child has asked to be called something different, this is one of the most concrete ways you can show support. You will make mistakes. What matters is that you try, that you correct yourself, and that your child sees you making the effort.

If you are not ready to use a new name or pronouns, consider intermediate steps. A gender-neutral nickname, using their first initial, or simply avoiding pronouns altogether while you adjust can help you stay respectful and connected as you find your footing.

Support self-expression. Clothing, hair, and style are ways young people explore identity. Remember that all adolescents experiment with appearance.

Help your child find community. Knowing other LGBTQ young people—or families like yours—can help your child feel less alone. Look for local support groups, school organizations, or online communities where they can connect with peers who understand their experience.

When You're Still Working Through Your Feelings

Strong feelings are natural. You may feel fear, grief, confusion, or relief. These feelings are valid, and you deserve support as you work through them. But your feelings and your parenting can be separate. You can feel overwhelmed and still show up with love. What matters is not asking your child to carry your emotions for you.

Parents often worry about safety, discrimination, relationships, and the future they imagined for their child. These fears come from love. Start by listening. Separate concerns about your child's wellbeing from worries about discomfort or public perception. Express fears as yours, not as facts about your child.

What helps most is separating fear from reality. Many LGBTQ people today build loving relationships, raise children, and live full lives. Your child's path may look different from what you expected, but different is not lesser.

Your child needs to know that your love for them is bigger than your uncertainty about their journey.

You can have questions and still be loving. You can move slowly and still stay close. What matters is that your child never has to wonder whether you are on their side.

Many parents eventually come to see that this part of their child's journey, while unexpected, deepened their own capacity for empathy, humility, and love. Not because the path was easy, but because their child invited them to grow. In this way, our children often become gifts to us, not in spite of who they are, but because of it.

When LGBTQ young people have accepting families, they live joyful, authentic lives. Your love makes this possible. It is the greatest gift you can give.

Stephanie Brill is the founder of Gender Spectrum and the author of *The Transgender Child* and *The Transgender Teen*, books that have guided hundreds of thousands of families through unfamiliar territory with love and practical wisdom. For over two decades, she has worked with parents from all backgrounds and belief systems, helping them stay connected to their children. She lives with the firm conviction that family love is the most powerful protective factor in any young person's life. Learn more and find resources for families at genderspectrum.org.

STAYING CONNECTED WITH YOUR LGBTQ TEEN

By Kateri Aninwood

Twenty-five percent of Gen Z identifies as LGBTQ.[24] That means our tweens and teens are growing up in a different world that has more gender diversity than the one we grew up in.

We have three young adult children. One is trans, one is gay, and one is exploring their sexual orientation. And we've learned a few things over the years, especially with our trans kid, that might be useful to you, too. But even if you don't have teens who are LGBTQ, chances are that you know some teens who are (even if they aren't "out" to you). Maybe they've visited your house, maybe they're your friend's kid, or your kid's friend. And the more we know how to support these teens—and all teens—the more we can create a kind and gentle world for all people.

I'm not an expert in the LGBTQ field. I'm just a mom with a story to share, and I hope it makes things a little easier for you.

[A quick note about names and pronouns to avoid confusion: In the transgender community, it is conventional to use someone's current name, gender, and pronouns even when referring to them in the past before they transitioned. I stuck to this convention here. Our trans child was identified female at birth and currently uses They/He pronouns.]

LGBTQ Kids Can Come from Wonderful Parents

My husband and I have been very intentional parents. Our kids grew up in a tight-knit, loving school. We raised our kids surrounded by extended family and community, at the school and the Catholic church that we attended for many years. We taught our kids that they have a voice, that they are powerful, and that we all need to care for people who are less fortunate and get along with others.

Each of our three kids developed their own personality within this environment. Our oldest was the "solid one," a responsible, thoughtful child who followed the rules and also had healthy boundaries. He was the "good friend" and the "gentle soul" who flourished through childhood. There were a few bumps in the road, but our oldest thrived; did well in school, wasn't overly influenced by media, and didn't have major mental health issues. As he grew up, he was a leader in sports, school, and in our community. Our oldest was also the one who came out as trans later on.

And we're not alone in this. For almost two decades, I've been friends with several parents who have trans kids or teens. They are wonderful, insightful, and kind parents with supportive families. They work as physicians, therapists, teachers, lawyers, architects, non-profit workers, designers, mathematicians, city workers, and artists. Their kids are doing great.

Sometimes Family Is Supportive—Sometimes They Need Time

When our oldest went off to college, they changed their pronouns to "They/Them" and told us that they were non-binary. Our oldest explained that the boxes of male and female just felt too confining. We were a little surprised by all of this—our child hadn't expressed difficulty with gender to us before then—but this was our solid, thoughtful, not impulsive kid. We didn't know if it would be a phase or not, but we were okay letting our oldest explore, experiment, try things on, figure things out, and trust in the process.

We could tell that using new pronouns was important to our child, so we did our best.

It felt grammatically awkward to use "They/Them" pronouns at first. It took practice for the words to flow.

Later in college, our son came out as transgender. Some of our extended family are accepting. Some extended family members are still struggling and don't completely understand. We continue to try to talk to them. Especially when our child came out, I didn't realize that I—not my child—would need to continue to explain things to our extended family. Family members would ask me the things they didn't feel like they could ask him. I didn't realize I would need to defend our child, and sometimes even have to defend our parenting. Not all of our relatives know trans people, and not everyone knows trans people who are thriving and living their best lives, so they had worries and concerns. It was new ground for them.

There have also been small miracles. A member of our family told their family doctor about our child being trans, and the doctor said, "Just love them." I also heard a family story that I had never heard before about a trans ancestor who lived generations ago.

"Coming Out" Is a Sign of the Strength of the Relationship

What I understand now is that anytime a child "comes out" to a parent, they know they are risking their relationship, risking the parent's love and acceptance. An LGBTQ person knows that they might be rejected by their family, friends, church, or community. They've already decided that the risk and pain of not being truly known is worse than the risk of being rejected. And yet, within that risk is also a profound statement of trust.

When our child came out to other family members and us, he didn't use these exact words, but his message was, "My 'coming out' is a sign of the strength of our relationship, our connection, that I feel safe enough telling you this about me rather than trying to hide it—and myself—from you." Coming out to another person is a tender and vulnerable gift.

Is Being Trans a "Social Contagion"?

Some people think that being trans is the result of social media and a social contagion. For our child, this didn't seem to be the case. He wasn't a heavy user of social media; he'd delete his accounts occasionally when he wanted a break. He appreciated some of the viewpoints he found from LGBTQ people on various platforms, which gave him language to describe his experience and made him feel less alone.

Social media is a complicated place for teens to be, in general. The algorithm can serve up healthy information or negative or unhealthy stuff. But for our child, we don't believe it "put ideas in his head"; rather, it gave him words to express the ideas that were already in his head.

Connection is Protective

When our child came out to us, I was acutely aware that suicide rates are much higher for transgender teens than for typical teens.[25] My reading of the research reinforced that family and community support and acceptance of trans kids is protective. Research suggests that family and community support can lower the rate of suicide for trans kids, perhaps even to levels comparable to those of typical kids.[26]

In addition to increased suicide risk, transgender folks are vulnerable in a lot of ways. They might experience discrimination or more questioning while going through security at the airport, if they get pulled over by the police, or even when getting carded when going into a bar (especially if their name and gender on their identification cards don't match their appearance). While there is no evidence that trans folks are more likely to commit acts of violence, they are more likely to be victims of violence.[27] These are sometimes things that keep me up at night, and I work to see the world as a generally safe place for all kids.

Despite those fears, my support for our oldest was not much different than what we did for our other kids. My support was my calm presence, being curious, and asking questions. We talk about gender and about everything else in this wonderful and complicated world we inhabit. My support is being interested in their lives, showing up, and cheering for them at each milestone. Conversations about gender were only a small part of our connection.

Through college, our oldest continued truckin' along... going to school, making friends, playing sports, working on campus, taking on leadership roles, falling in—and out—of love, defending and supporting people who had less than he did, and learning how to juggle all the responsibilities and joys of life as a college student.

My Own Emotional Process

At various times, I was surprised, confused, and worried about our child. Sometimes I was grieving. But I was reassured by the solidness of my child, the deliberateness of their choices throughout their life. I was reassured by the slowness and thoughtfulness of their process.

Figuring out one's identity is a primary task during adolescence. Experimentation is to be expected. It was helpful to connect with the other parents we knew with non-binary or trans kids and to normalize our experience. I even now know a couple of trans elders—in their 70s—who shared their stories with us. But even as we had examples of other families working through this, it was still a lot to process at times.

I committed to doing my own emotional work, not in front of my child. That way, he didn't have to feel burdened with my emotions too, at the same time that he's trying to figure things out for himself. In fact, I've done the same thing with all of our kids. As much as I can, I do my own emotional work on my own. I believe that kids are more likely to talk to and open up to their parents if they don't feel responsible for their parents' feelings.

The Next Transition

After two years of college, our oldest changed their pronouns to "They/He" and their name from what we had called them since they were born. We continued having conversations, and we stayed close. He shared his goals for the future, his insights into himself, his friends, his classes, his work, and his life.

He had to wait for a couple of years for an opening at the large hospital in the "big city." He was 20 years old when we drove up together for the first time and met with a team of doctors who, with his therapist, talked to him about the pros and cons of various options, including the option of no intervention at all. No one pressured him. No one rushed him. No one favored one option over another. Some transgender people don't take hormones or take them for only a period of time; some trans folks choose not to have surgery. Every person is unique.

He was in charge of the process. We gathered the information together. And just like all the other possibly life-changing decisions that teens and young people make—college and what to major in, marriage, tattoos, sex and relationships, joining the military, driving, or voting—we trusted that he was in the best position to decide what would be best for him (not us). "You get to choose your life," we told him. "We'll love you either way," and we said, "This is not about us, this is about you."

Our Happy Ending

The past several years have had their ups and downs for sure. We haven't always been perfect parents for our trans kid, but we continue to have conversations, clear up the misunderstandings, and we've grown closer together as a family. After going through the grief and uncertainty, we've begun to celebrate. That celebration doesn't come with fireworks, grand gestures, or an audience; for us, it's more like the gentle, quiet beauty of the dawn or a flower blooming in spring.

When my dad's health was declining, our son "came out" to him. My dad, who had always been supportive of all our kids, said, "In nature, variety is the norm. Every owl, frog, and blade of grass is unique. We don't have to fit ourselves into a box to be loved by God. God loves us not in spite of our uniqueness, but because of it."

My dad's last words to our son before he died were, "I love you. You are special."

A year after he died, we went on a family reunion memorial trip to visit my dad's relatives in the rural Midwest. We didn't know what to expect, but our child was embraced, quite literally, with open arms. We saw family members, older and younger, conservative and liberal, some who knew our child before his transition, and some who were meeting him for the first time. They accepted our child. All three of our kids went with a large group of cousins to splash and swim in the lake together. Afterward, I asked our son, "How did it feel to be in your body while swimming in the lake?"

"I felt free," he said.

Kateri Aninwood is a dedicated mom of three kids who are now young adults. She has worked in healthcare and education for two decades. As a new empty nester, she now has more time to help others who are less fortunate, share her experience raising LGBTQ youth within a faith community, paint watercolors, and sit with her husband over a morning cup of coffee and a crossword. If you are looking for resources to support an LGBTQ youth in your life, scan the QR code to connect with PFLAG, a non-profit with virtual and in-person events, support groups, education, and advocacy.

ENDNOTES

Section One

1. John Gottman and Joan DeClaire, *Raising an Emotionally Intelligent Child: The Heart of Parenting* (New York: Simon & Schuster, 1997).

2. Daniel J. Siegel and Tina Payne Bryson, *The Whole-Brain Child: 12 Revolutionary Strategies to Nurture Your Child's Developing Mind* (New York: Bantam, 2011).

3. Mona Delahooke, *Brain-Body Parenting: How to Stop Managing Behavior and Start Raising Joyful, Resilient Kids* (New York: HarperOne, 2022).

4. Lisa Damour, "Gen Zers to Their Parents: When We Are Upset, Just Listen (New Gallup Poll)," drlisadamour.com, August 5, 2024, https://drlisadamour.com/resource/gen-zers-to-their-parents-when-we-are-upset-just-listen/.

Section Two

5. Morris, A. S., Silk, J. S., Steinberg, L., Myers, S. S., & Robinson, L. R. (2007). *"The role of the family context in the development of emotion regulation." Social Development 16(2): 361–388. https://doi. org/10.1111/j.1467-9507.2007.00389.x*

6. *"Emotion." Author manuscript; available in PMC: 2014 Sep 26. Published in final edited form as: Emotion10(6):923–933. doi: https://doi. org/10.1037/a0021156*

7. *Lopes, P. N., Salovey, P., Côté, S., Beers, M., & Petty, R. E. (2005). "Emotion regulation abilities and the quality of social interaction." Emotion 5(1): 113–118. https://doi.org/10.1037/1528-3542.5.1.113*

8. *Girotti, M., Adler, S. M., Bulin, S. E., Fucich, E. A., Paredes, D., & Morilak, D. A. (2017). "Prefrontal cortex executive processes affected by stress in health and disease." Progress in Neuro-Psychopharmacology & Biological Psychiatry 85: 161–179. https://doi.org/10.1016/j.pnpbp.2017.07.004*

Section Three

9. Ann & Robert H. Lurie Children's Hospital of Chicago. (2023, December). *Raising kids now: Millennial parenting styles.* Lurie Children's. https://www.luriechildrens.org/en/blog/millenni-al-parenting-statistics/

10. Méndez-Lara, Lessa A., Rodrigo Ramirez-Rodriguez, Edgar Santos, and Angel Puig-Lagunes. "Comparative Analysis of Stress Levels and Coping Strategies in Parents of Neurodivergent and

Neurotypical Children." *Frontiers in Child and Adolescent Psychiatry* 4 (2025): 1619993. https://doi.org/10.3389/frcha.2025.1619993.

11. Rosanbalm, Katie D., and Desiree W. Murray. "Caregiver Co-regulation Across Development: A Practice Brief." OPRE Brief #2017-80. Washington, DC: Office of Planning, Research and Evaluation, Administration for Children and Families, U.S. Department of Health and Human Services, October 2017. https://fpg.unc.edu/sites/fpg.unc.edu/files/resources/reports-and-policy-briefs/Co-RegulationFromBirthThrough-YoungAdulthood.pdf.

12. World Health Organization, "Suicide," World Health Organization, March 2025, https://www.who.int/news-room/fact-sheets/detail/suicide.

Section Four

13. KFF. "Sex Education Programs: Definitions, Funding, and Impact on Teen Sexual Health." October 30, 2025. https://www.kff.org/womens-health-policy/sex-education-programs-definitions-funding-and-impact-on-teen-sexual-health/. The Trevor Project. "Acceptance from Adults is Associated with Lower Rates of Suicide Attempts Among LGBTQ Young People." 2023. https://www.thetrevorproject.org/research-briefs/acceptance-from-adults-is-associated-with-lower-rates-of-suicide-attempts-among-lgbtq-young-people-sep-2023/.

14. Feijoo, Ammie N. "Adolescent Sexual Health in Europe and the U.S.—Why the Difference?" Advocates for Youth, 2001. https://www.advocatesforyouth.org/wp-content/uploads/storage/advfy/documents/adolescent_sexual_health_in_europe_and_the_united_states.pdf.

15. Common Sense Media. *Teens and Pornography*. San Francisco: Common Sense Media, January 10, 2023. https://www.commonsensemedia.org/research/teens-and-pornography.

16. Minihan, Savannah, Melanie Burton, Katherine Giunta, Laureen Villegas, and Mariesa Nicholas. "Young People's Intentional and Unintentional Encounters with Internet Pornography in Australia." *Archives of Sexual Behavior* 54, no. 4 (April 2025): 1575–1588. https://doi.org/10.1007/s10508-025-03109-2.

17. Centers for Disease Control and Prevention, "Youth Risk Behavior Survey Data Summary & Trends Report: 2013–2023" (U.S. Department of Health and Human Services, 2024), https://www.cdc.gov/yrbs/dstr/index.html.

18. ElSohly, M. A., Mehmedic, Z., Foster, S., Gon, C., Chandra, S., & Church, J. C. (2016). Changes in cannabis potency over the last two decades (1995–2014). Biological Psychiatry, 79(7), 613–619. *https://doi.org/10.1016/j.biopsych.2016.01.004*

19. Lubman, Dan I., Alexandra Cheetham, and Murat Yücel. "Cannabis and Adolescent Brain Development." Pharmacology & Therapeutics 148 (2015): 1–16.

20. National Institute on Drug Abuse. "Marijuana Drug Facts." Accessed February 28, 2026. *https://nida.nih.gov/publications/drugfacts/marijuana.*

21. Roehler, Douglas R., et al. "Cannabis-Involved Emergency Department Visits Among Persons Aged ‹25 Years Before and During the COVID-19 Pandemic—United States, 2019–2022." Morbidity and Mortality Weekly Report 72, no. 28 (July 14, 2023): 758–65. *https://www.cdc.gov/mmwr/volumes/72/wr/mm7228a1.htm.*

22. Silins, Edmund, et al. "Young Adult Sequelae of Adolescent Cannabis Use: An Integrative Analysis." The Lancet Psychiatry 1, no. 4 (September 2014): 286–93. *https://doi.org/10.1016/S2215-0366(14)70307-4.*

23. Meyers, Robert J., Hendrik G. Roozen, and Jane Ellen Smith. "The Community Reinforcement Approach: An Update of the Evidence." Alcohol Research & Health 33, no. 4 (2011): 380–88.

Section Six

24. Carter Sherman, *The Second Coming: Sex and the Next Generation's Fight Over Its Future* (New York: Gallery Books, 2025), 118.

25. Ann P. Haas, Philip L. Rodgers, and Jody L. Herman, "Suicide Attempts Among Transgender and Gender Non-Conforming Adults: Findings of the National Transgender Discrimination Survey" (American Foundation for Suicide Prevention and The Williams Institute, UCLA School of Law, 2014), quoted in Stephanie Brill and Lisa Kenney, *The Transgender Teen* (San Francisco: Cleis Press, 2016), 143.

26. R. Travers, G. Bauer, J. Pyne, K. Bradley, L. Gale, and M. Papadimitriou, "Impacts of Strong Parental Support for Trans Youth" (Trans PULSE Project, 2012), *http://transpulseproject.ca/research/impacts-of-strong-parental-support-for-trans-youth/*, quoted in Stephanie Brill and Lisa Kenney, *The Transgender Teen* (Berkeley: Cleis Press, 2016), 228.

27. Abels, Grace "There's No Evidence of Rising LGBTQ+ Violent Extremism or 'Trans Terrorism,'" Poynter, February 27, 2024, https://www.poynter.org/fact-checking/2024/mass-shoot-ings-caused-by-trans-lgbtq-people/.